SUGAR SKULLS

COLORING BOOK

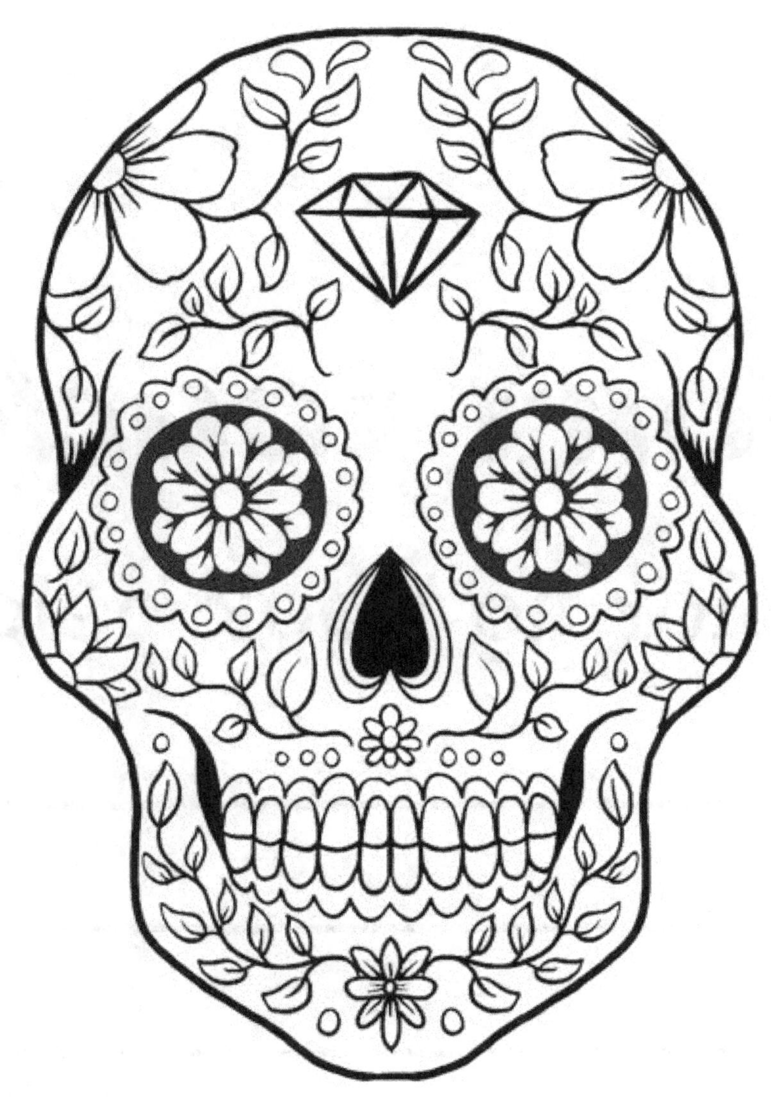

Don't touch!

This coloring book belong to:

____

____

____

TEST COLOR PAGE

TEST COLOR PAGE

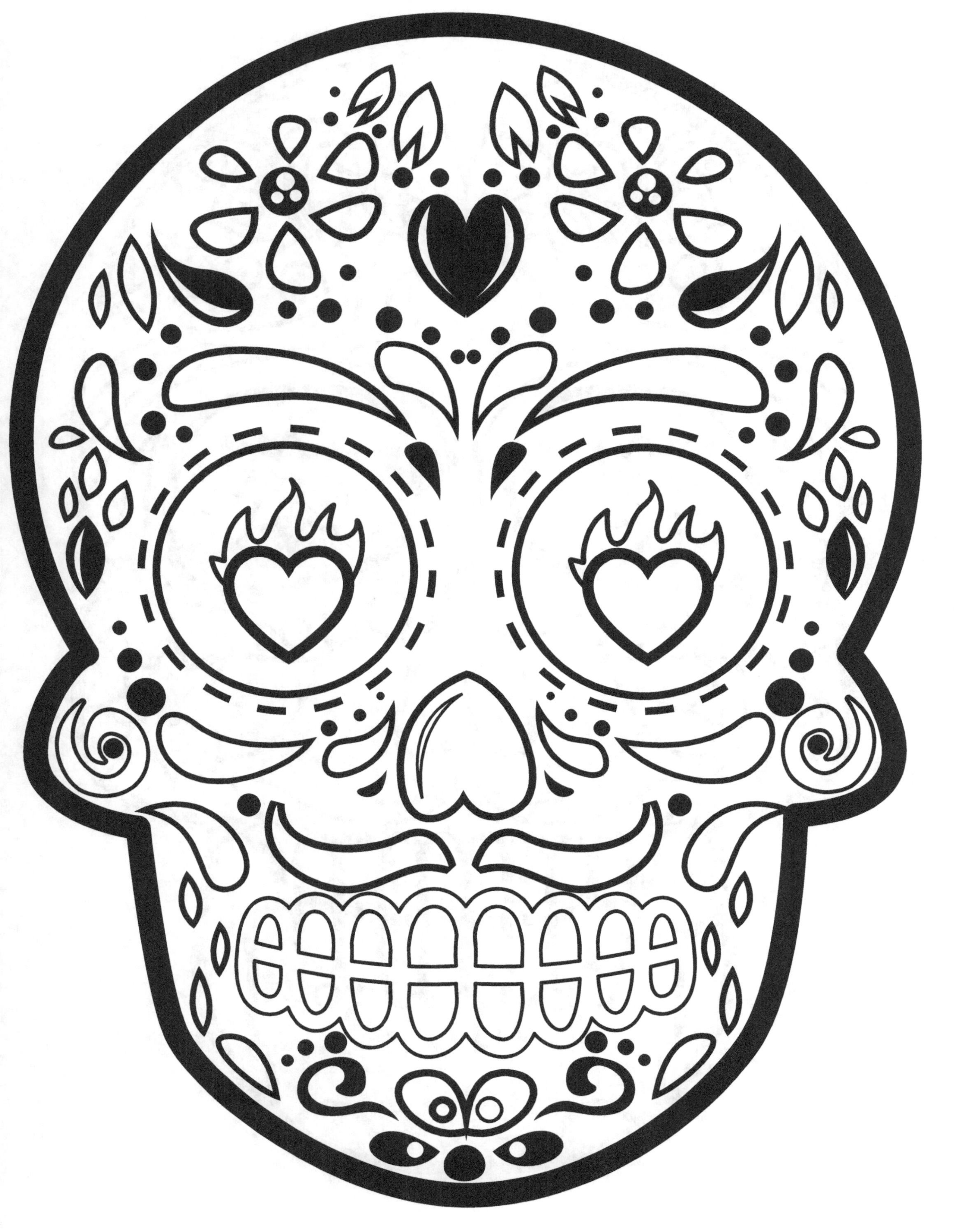

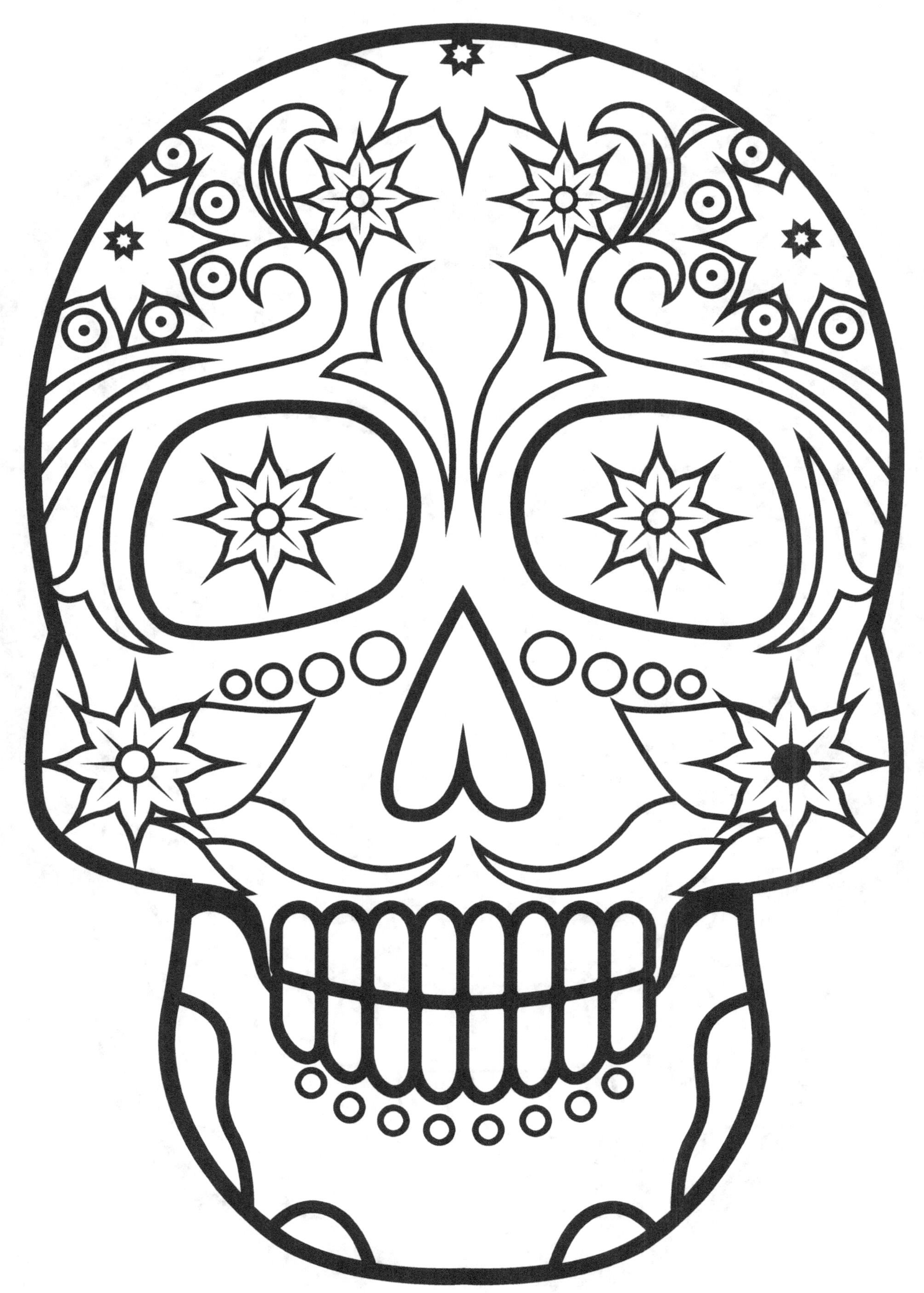

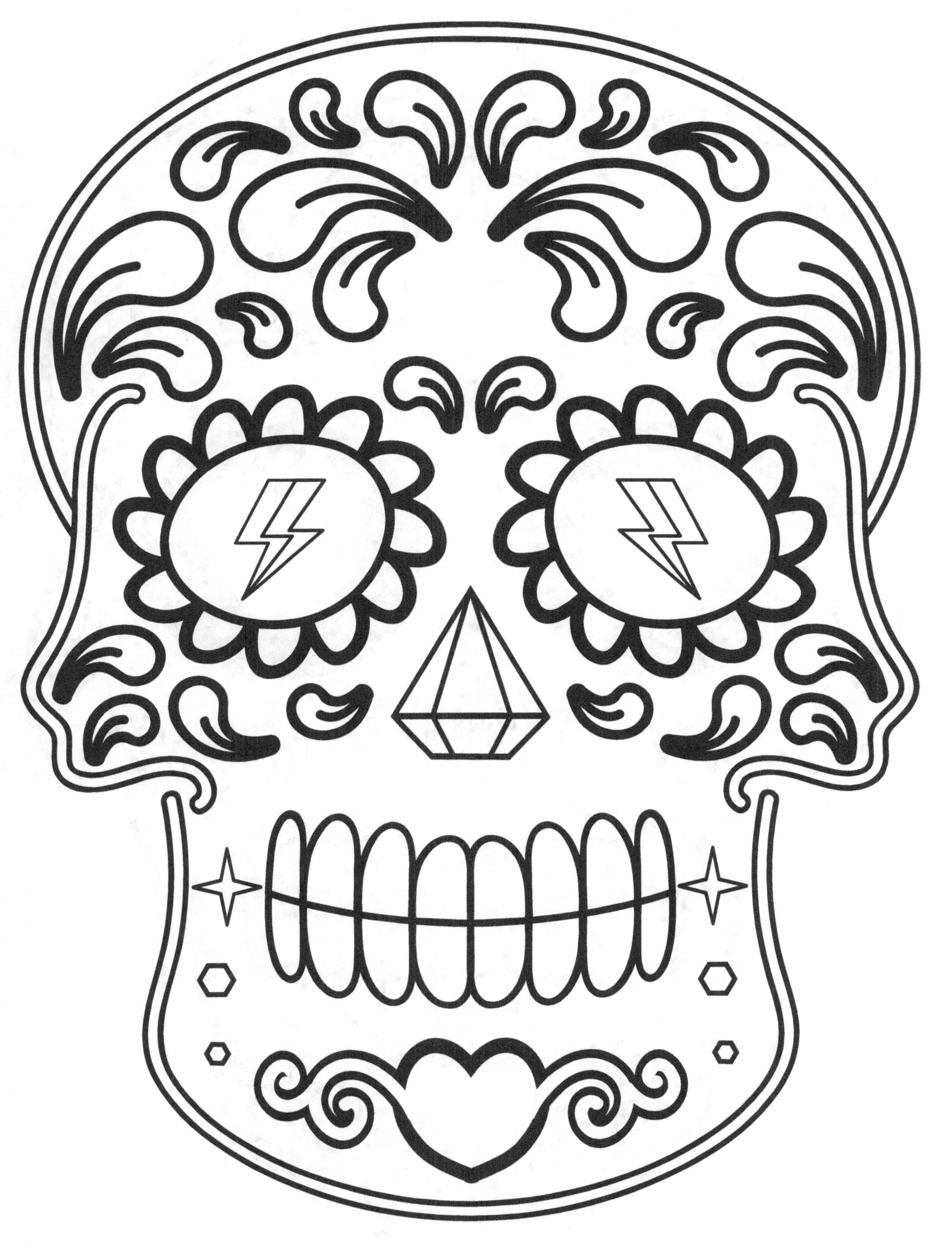

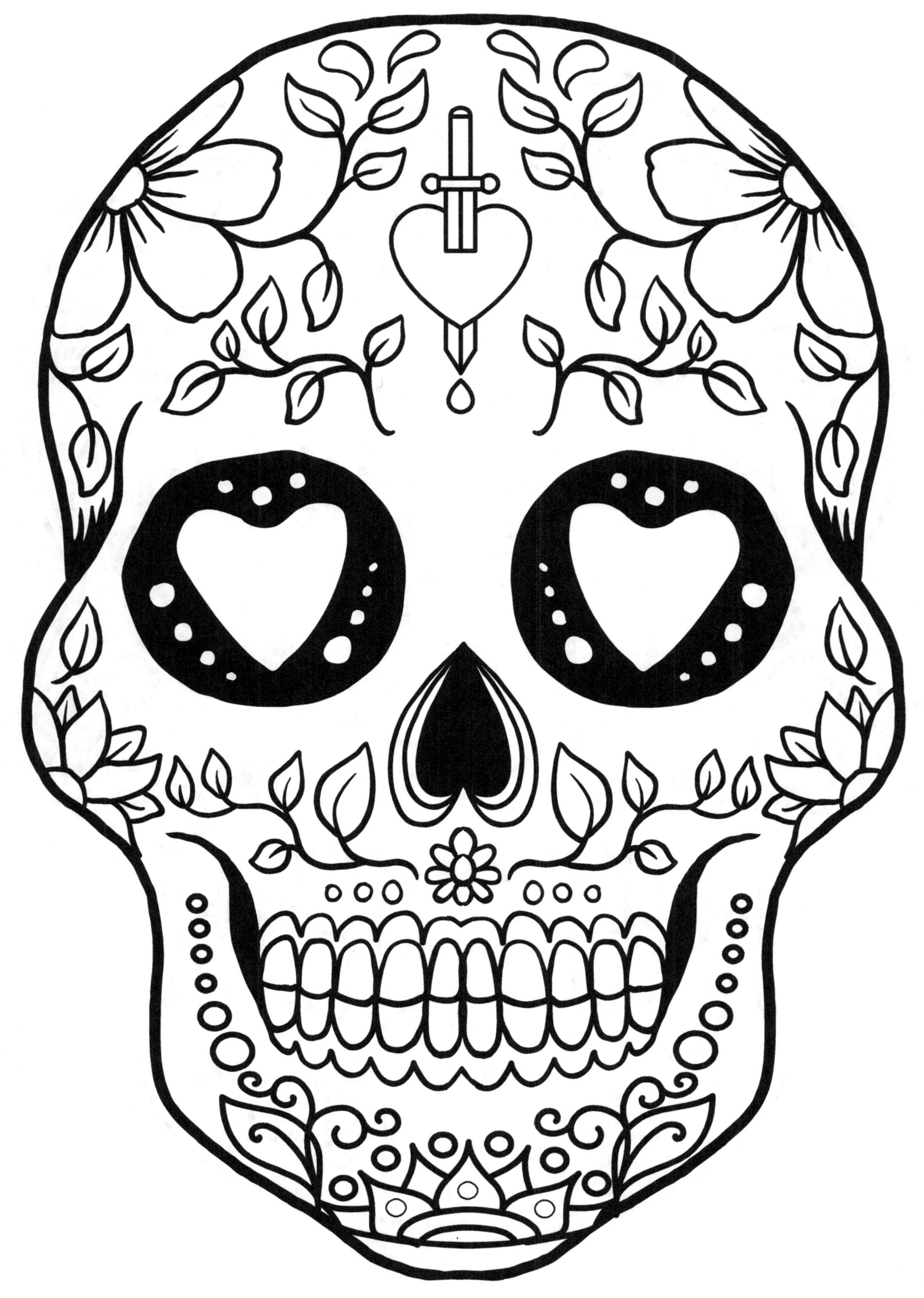

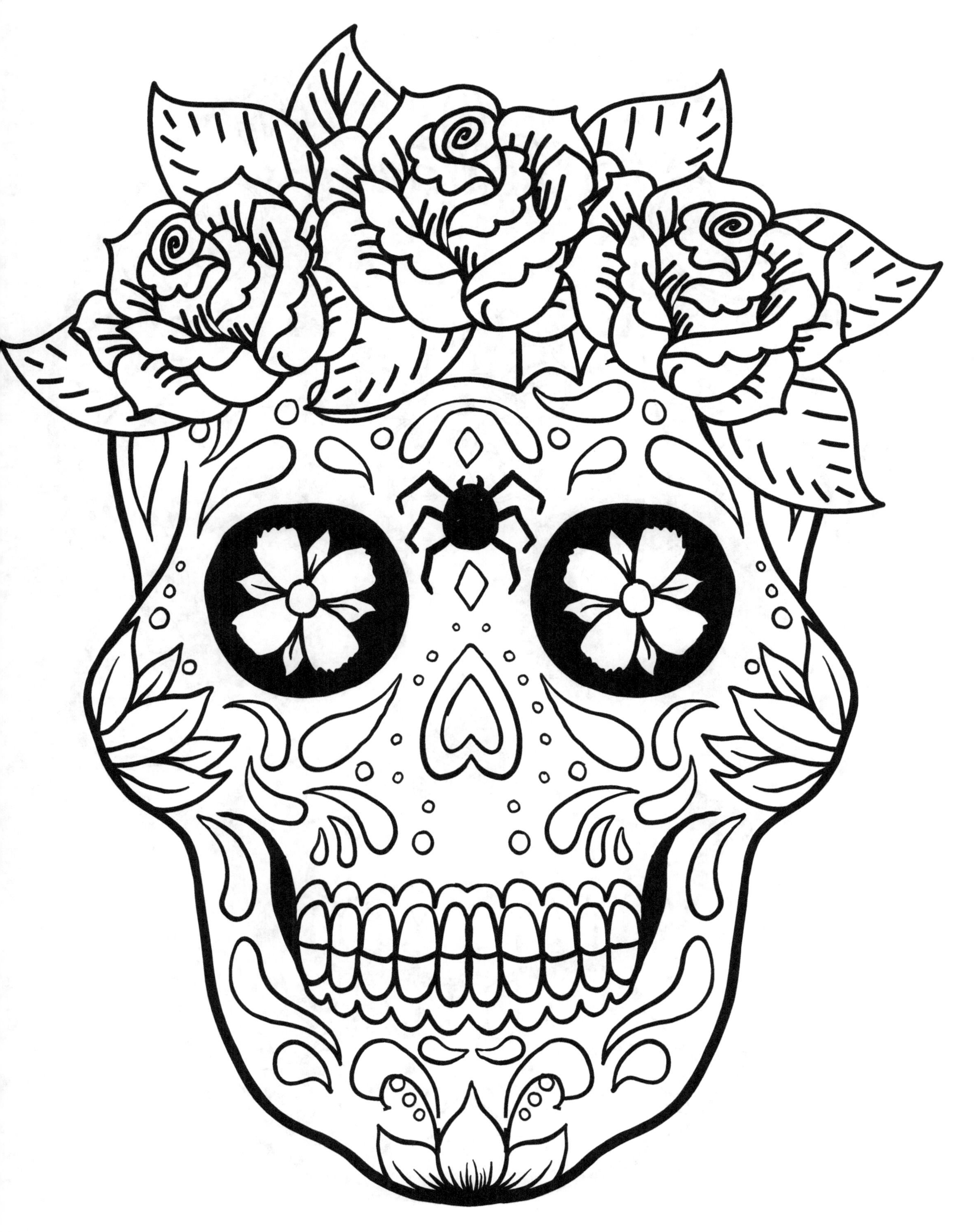

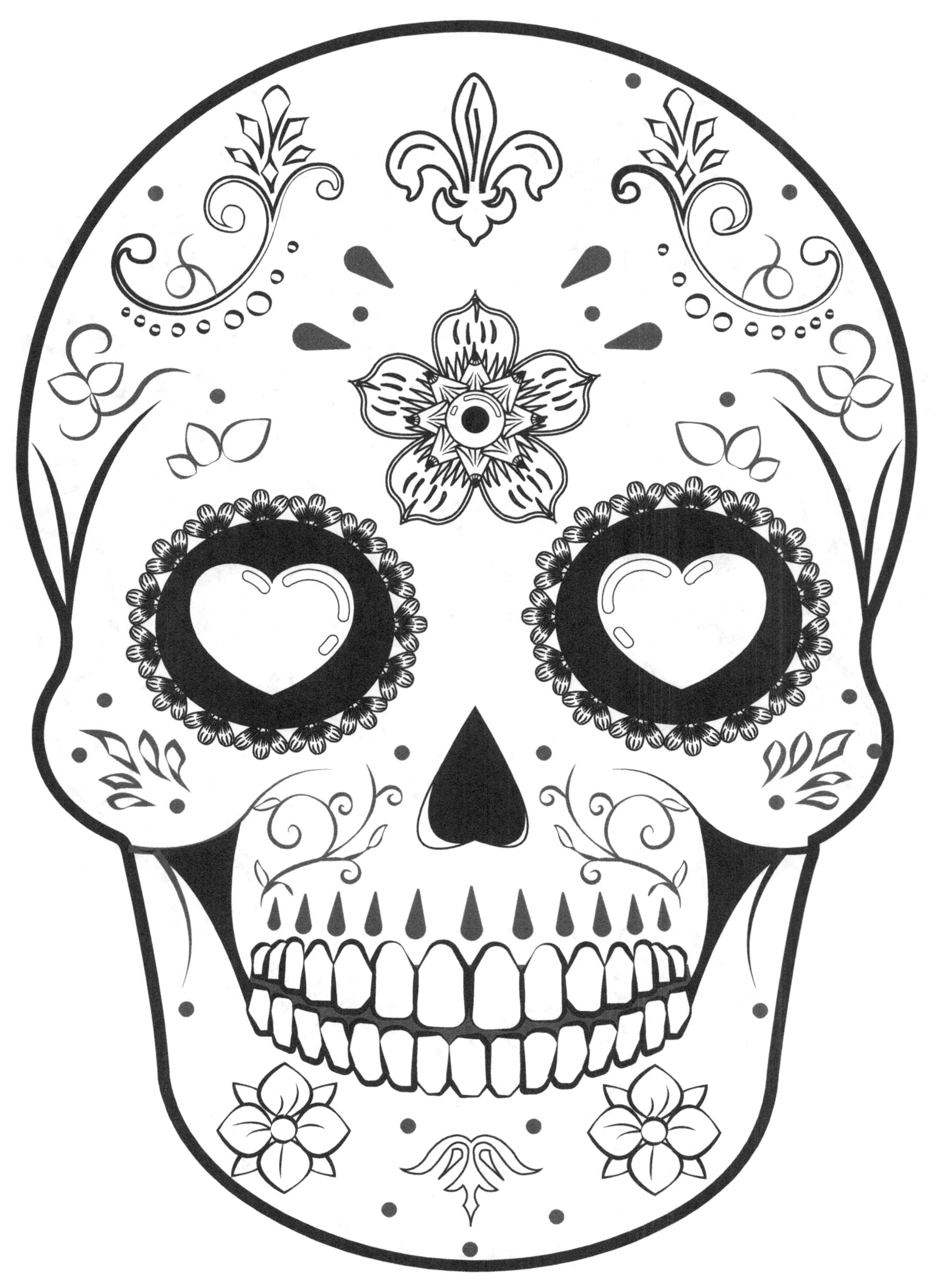

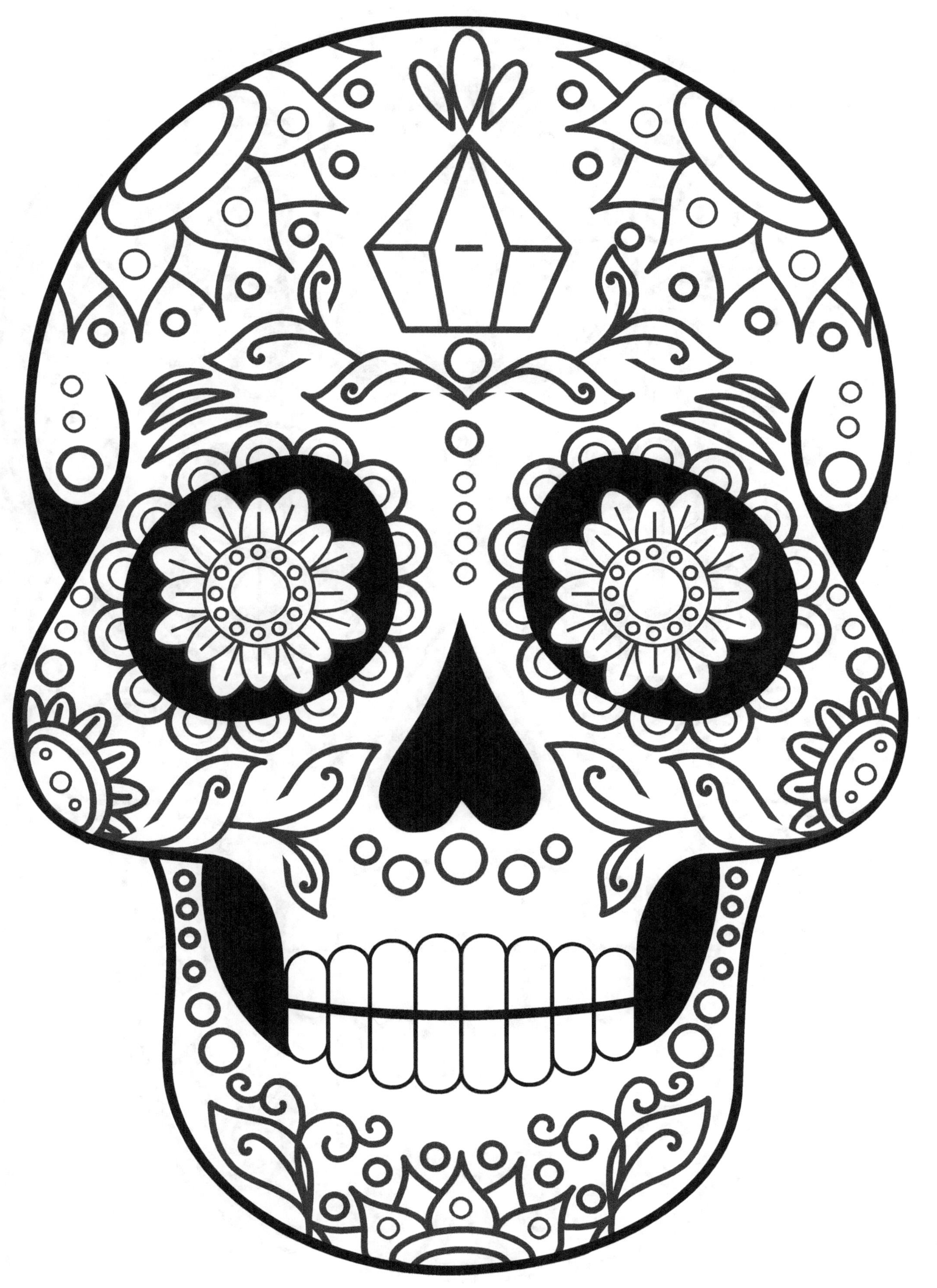

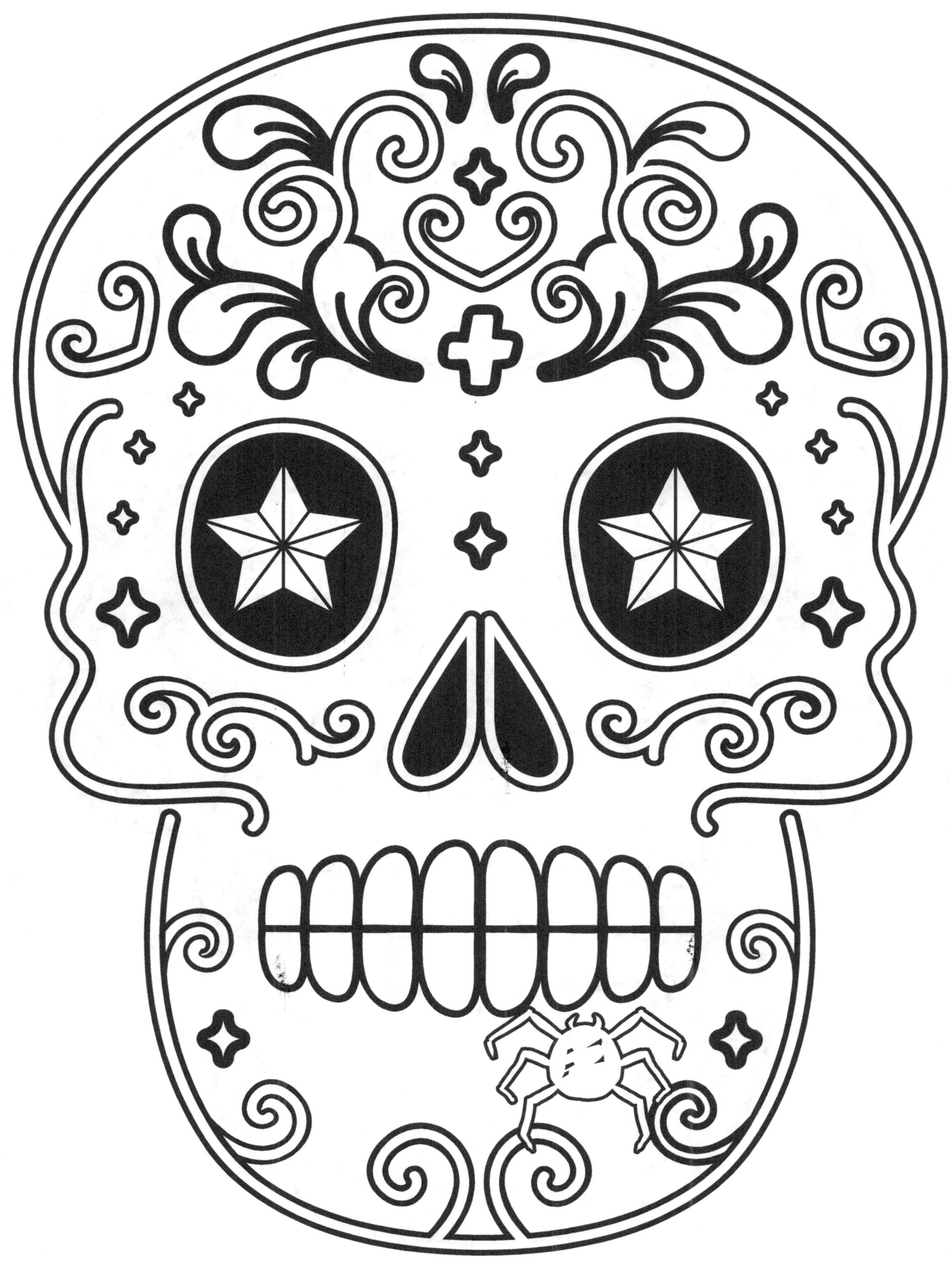

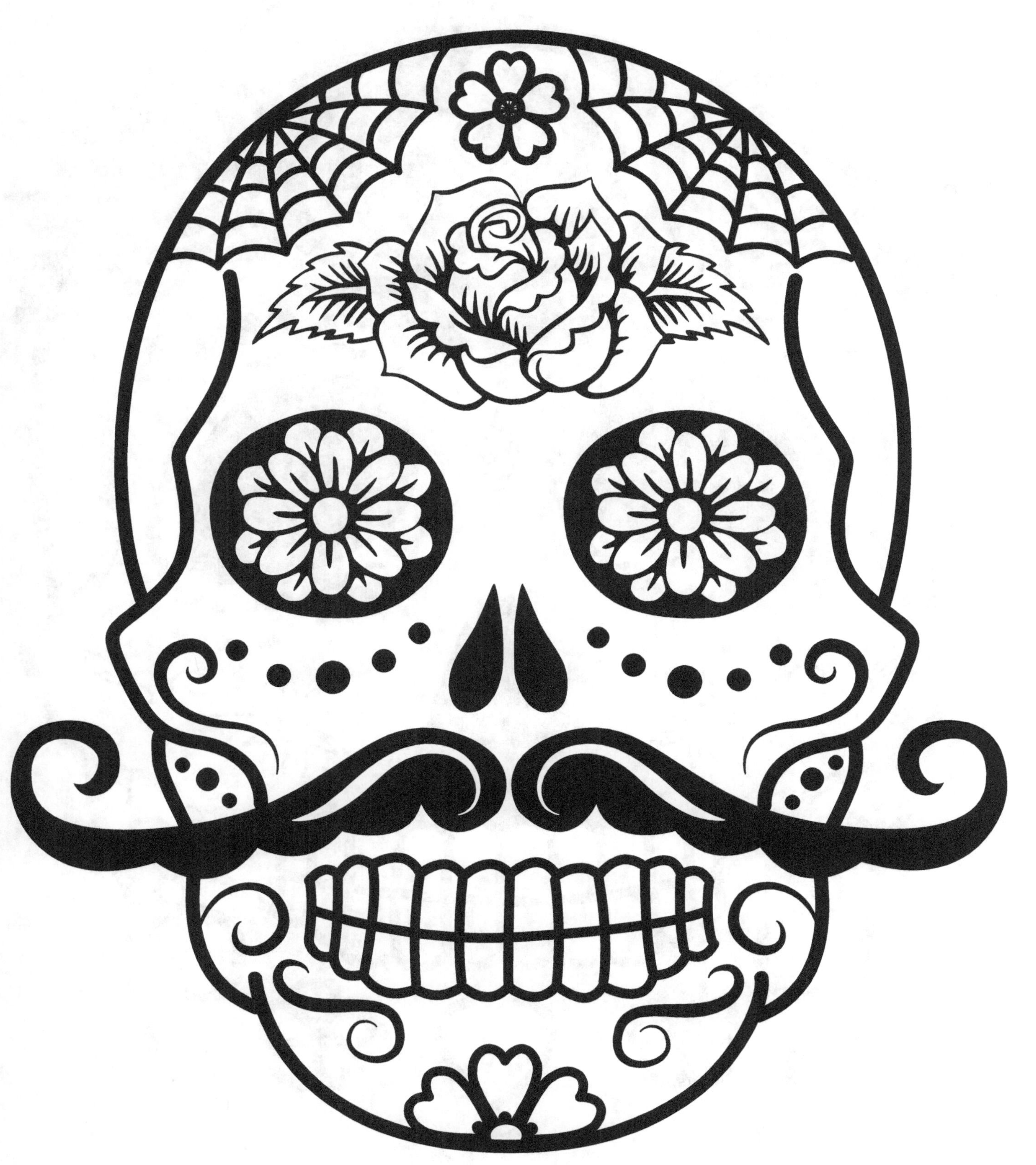

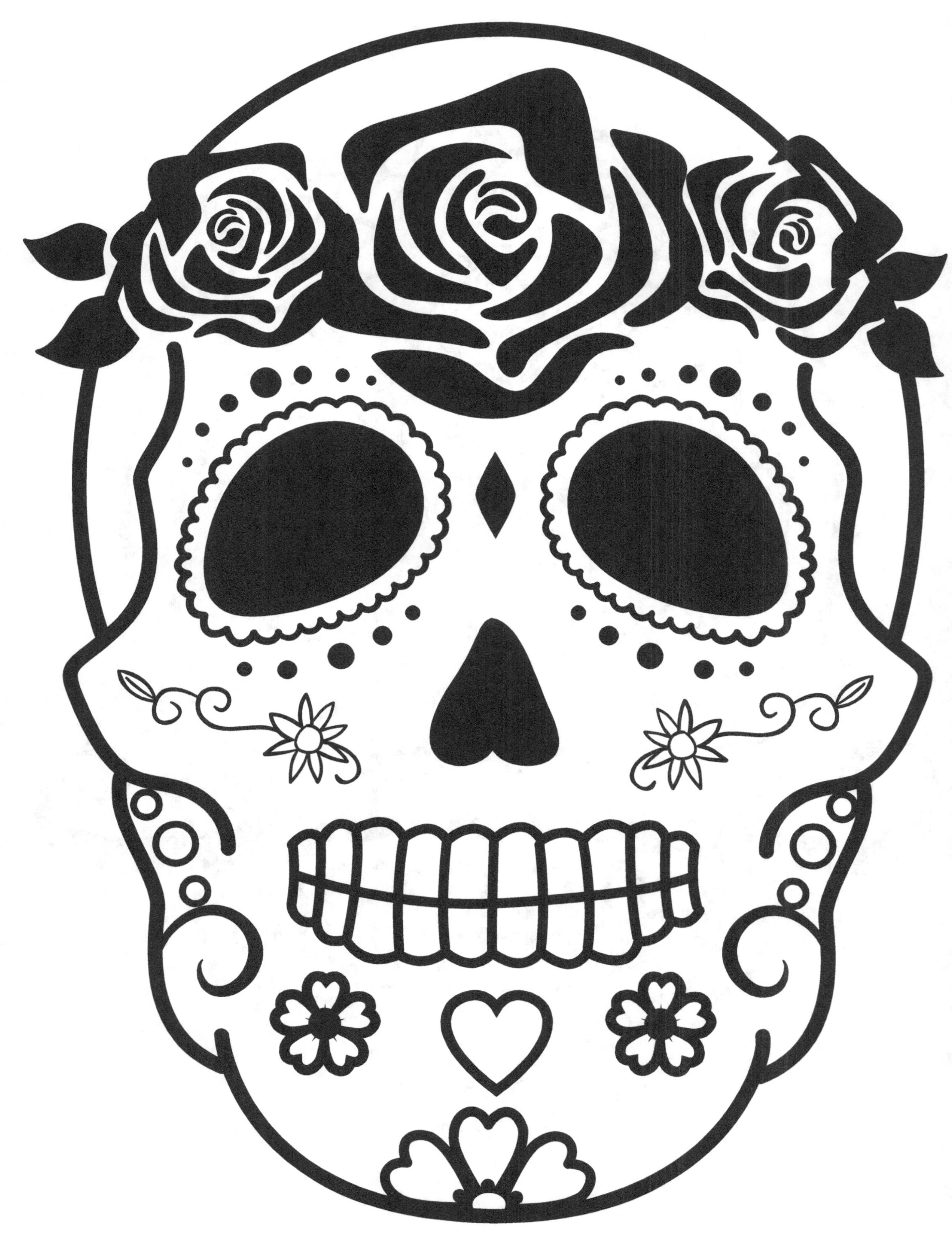

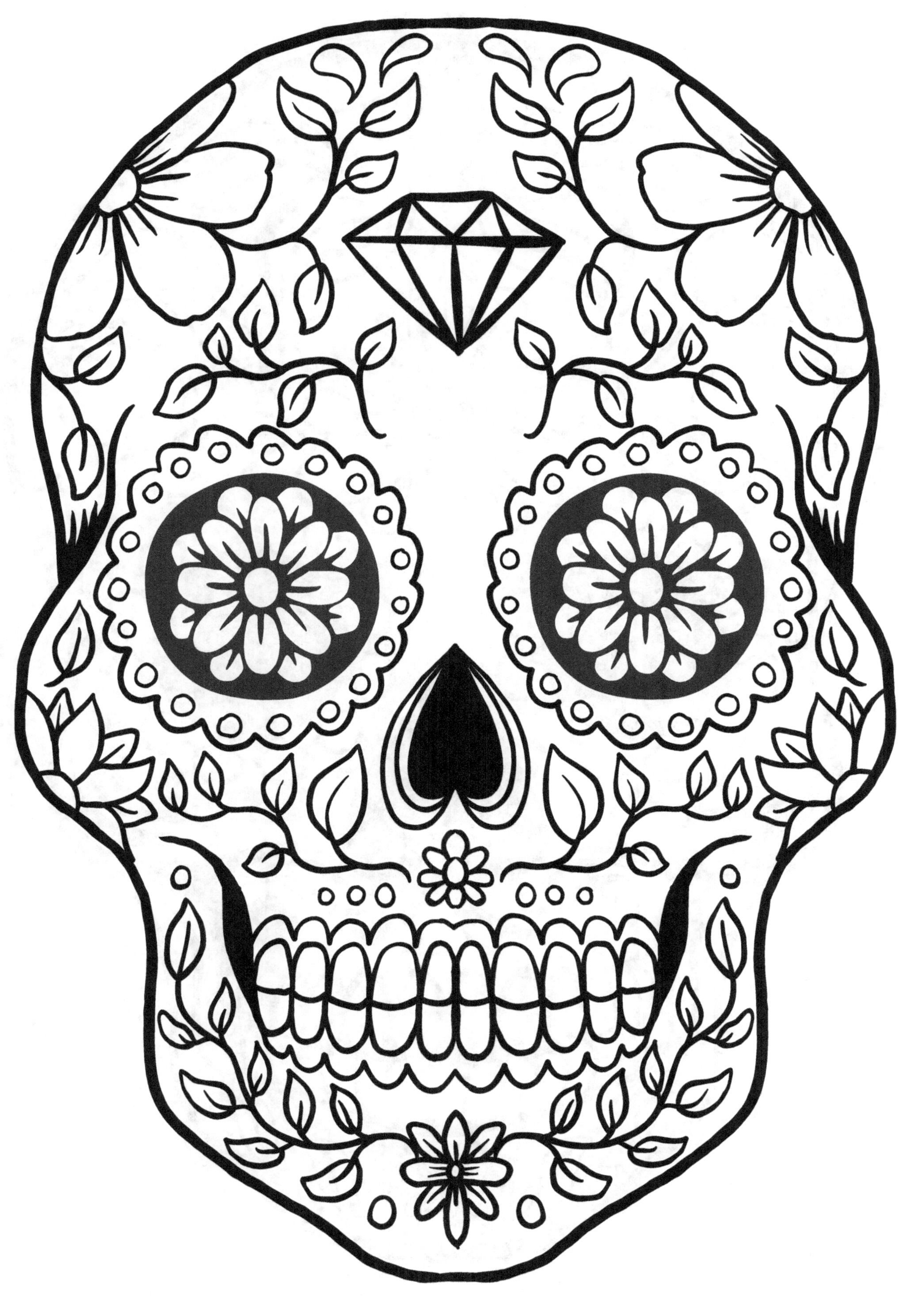

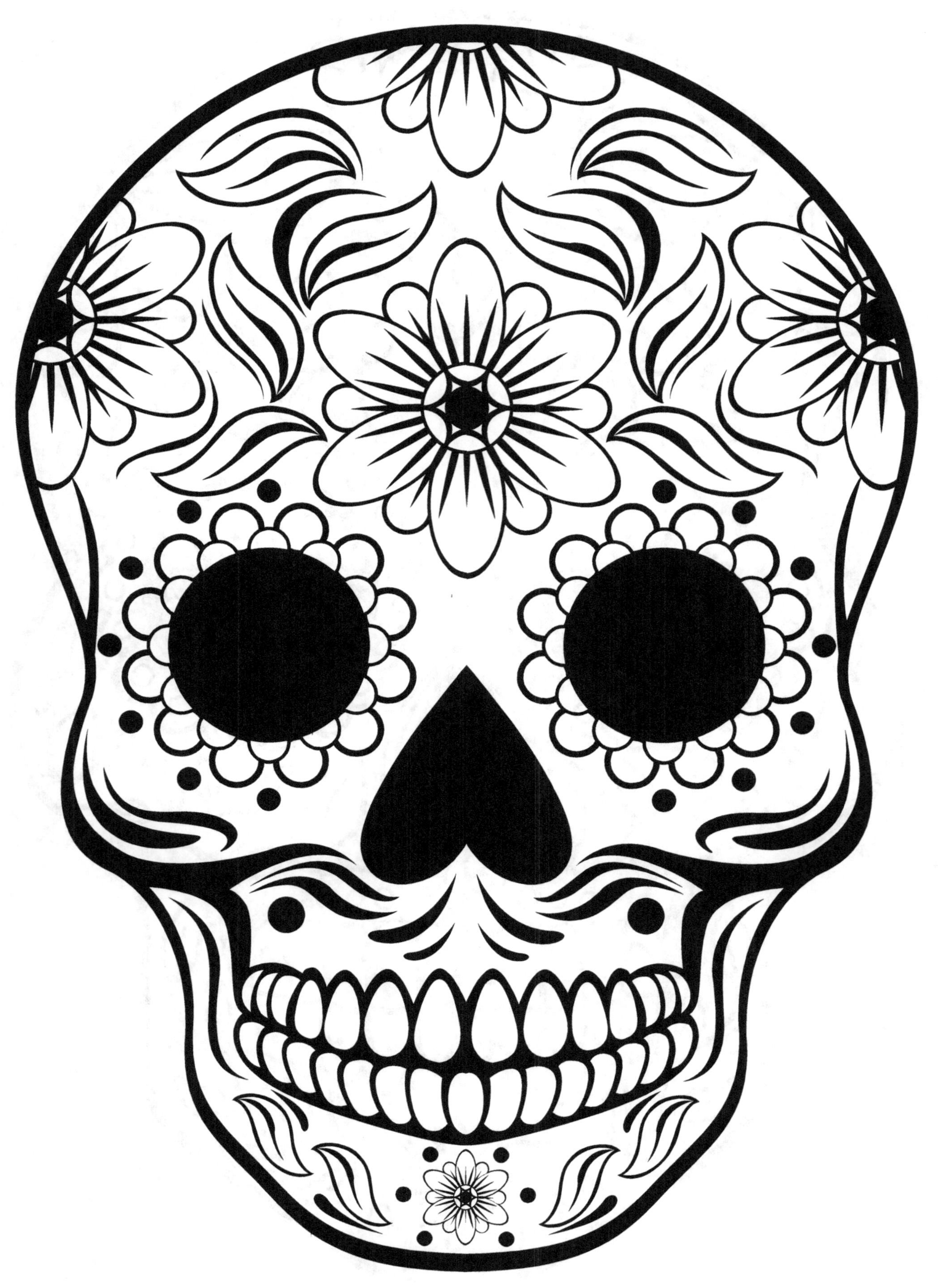

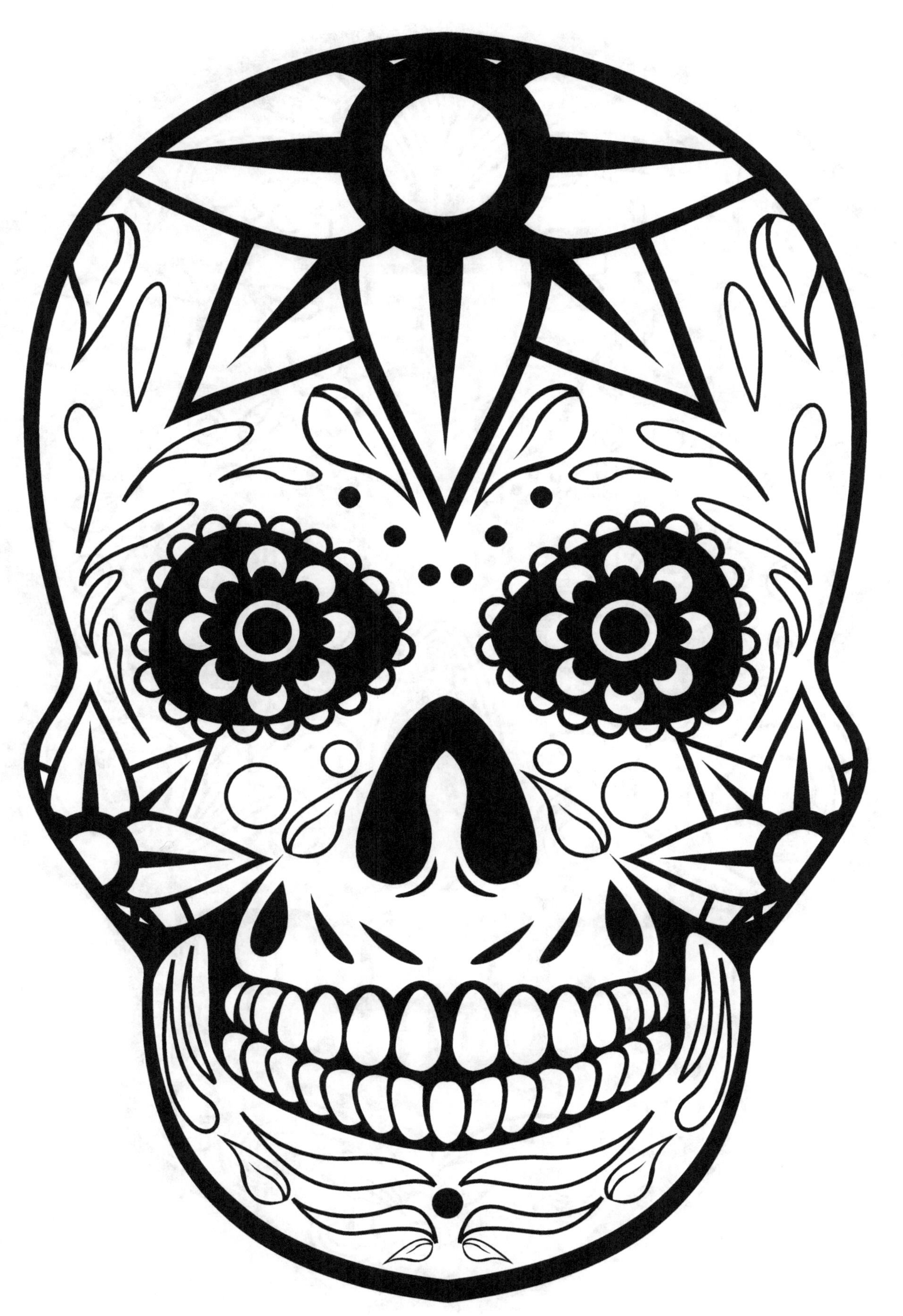

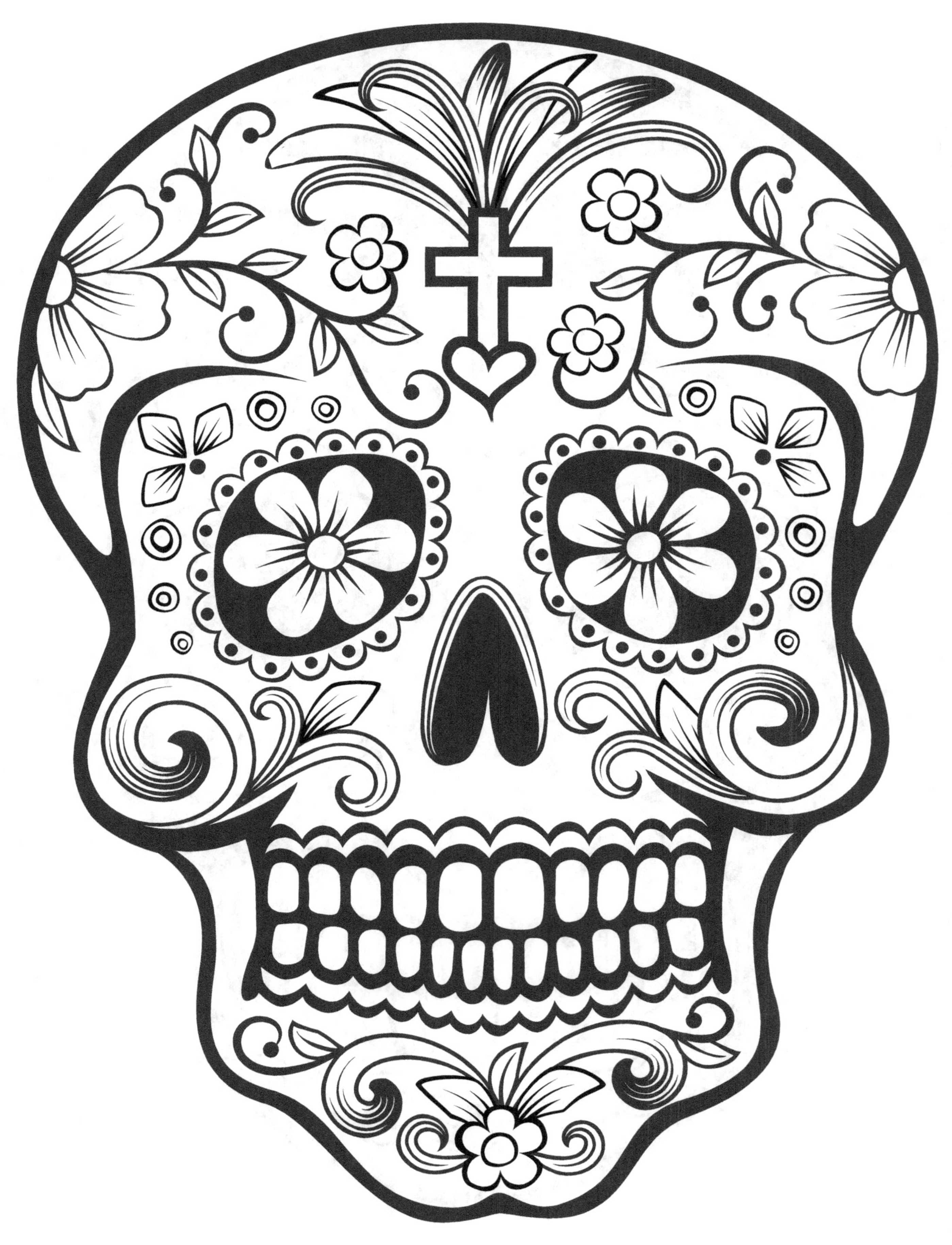

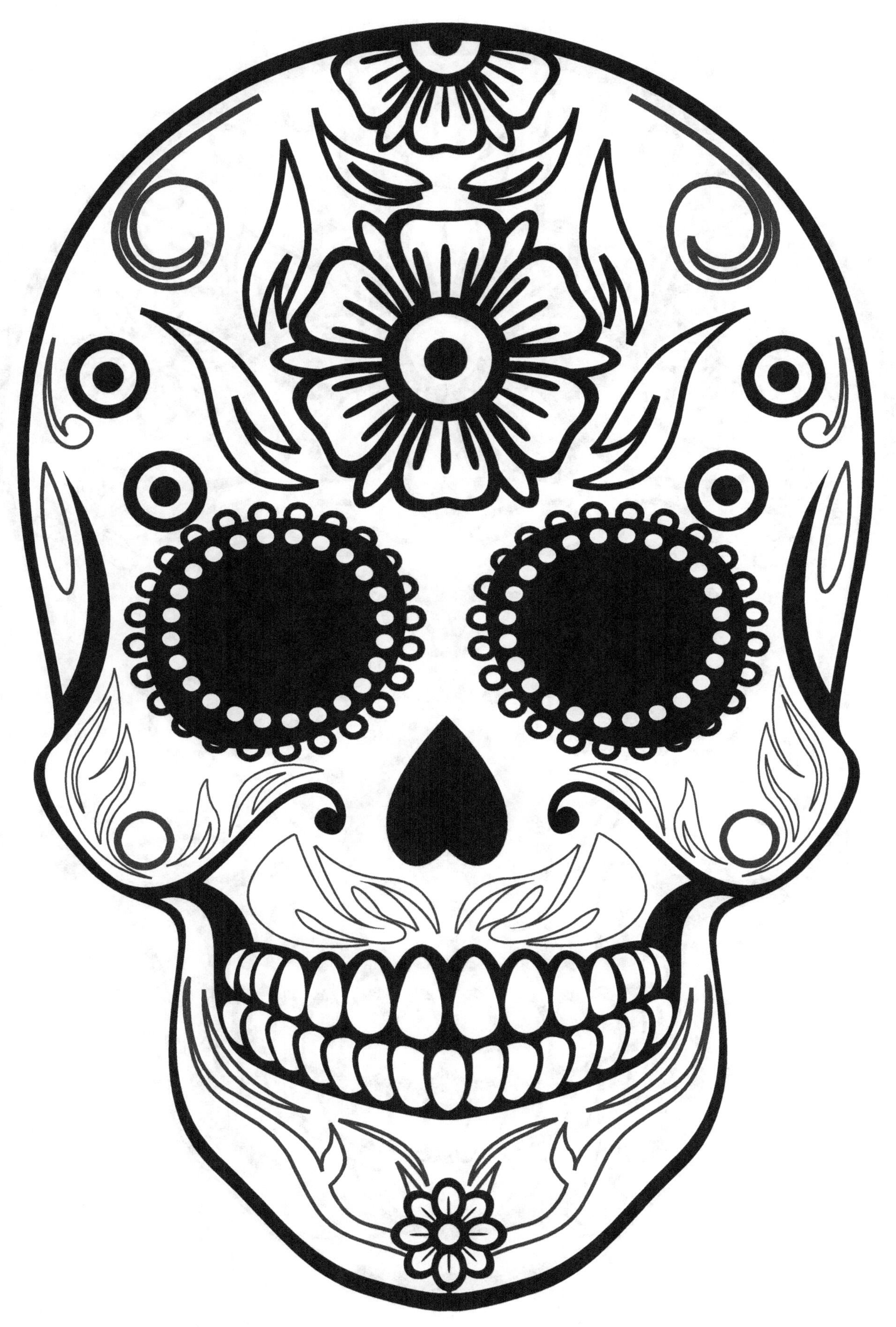

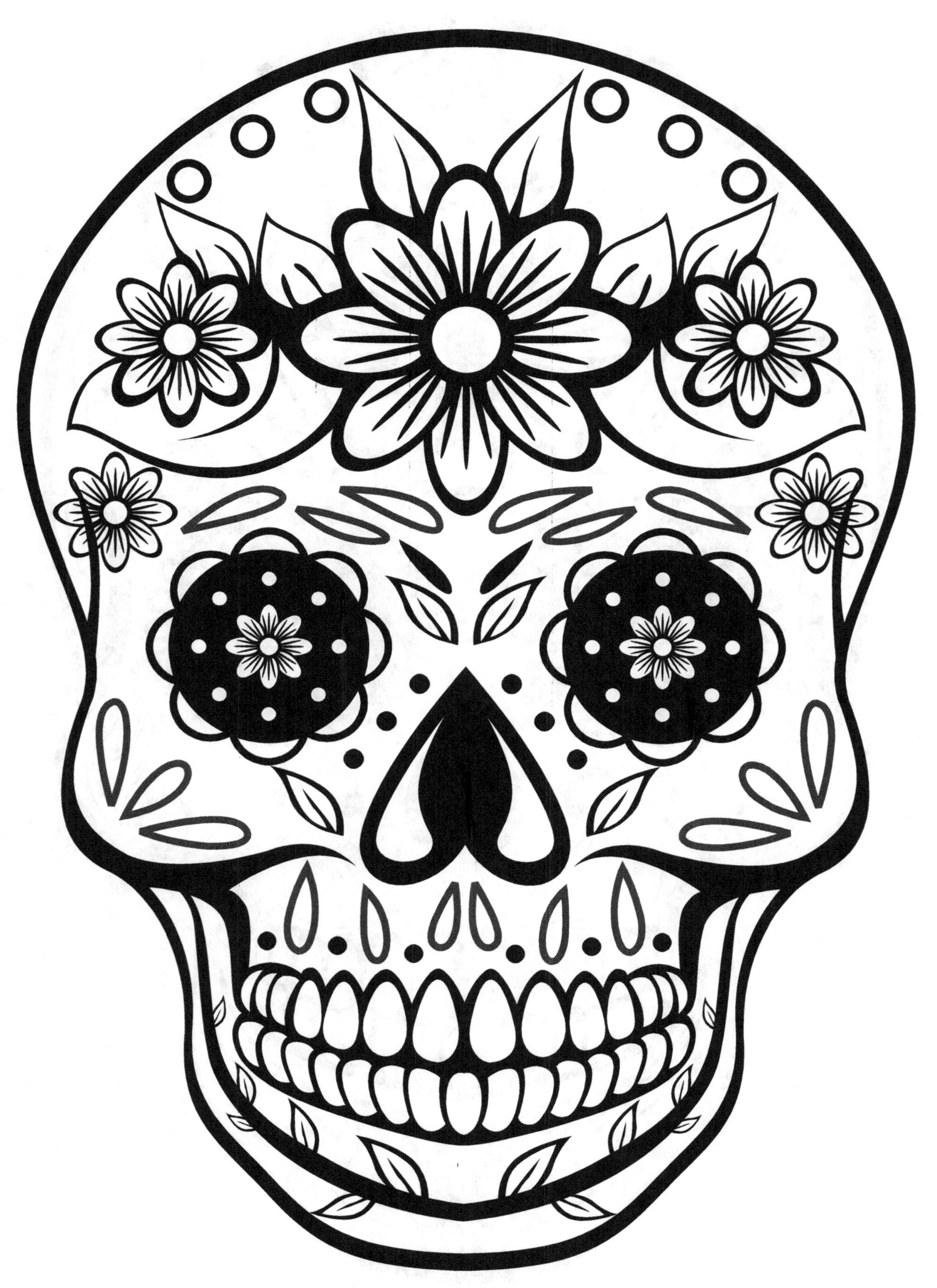

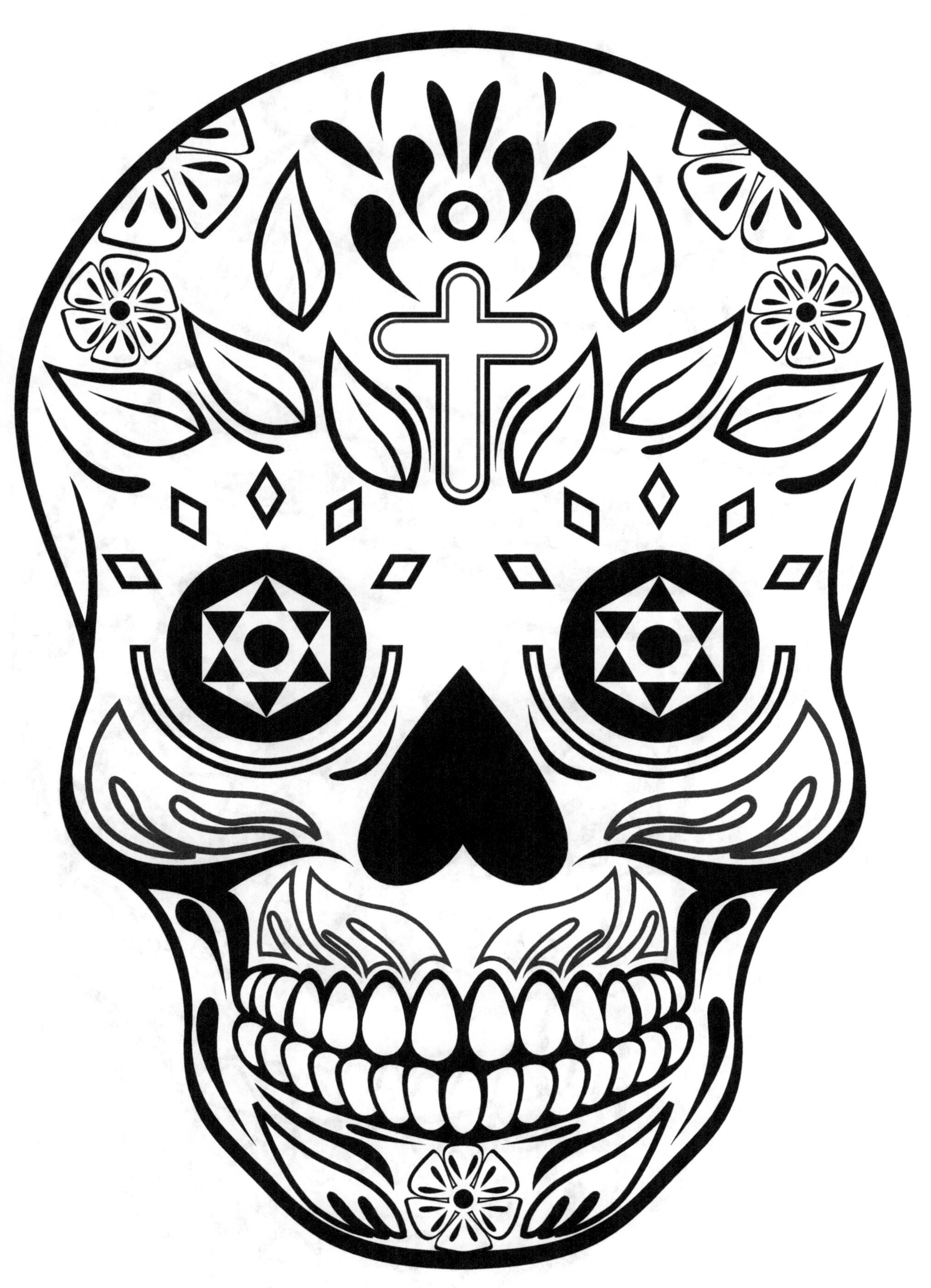

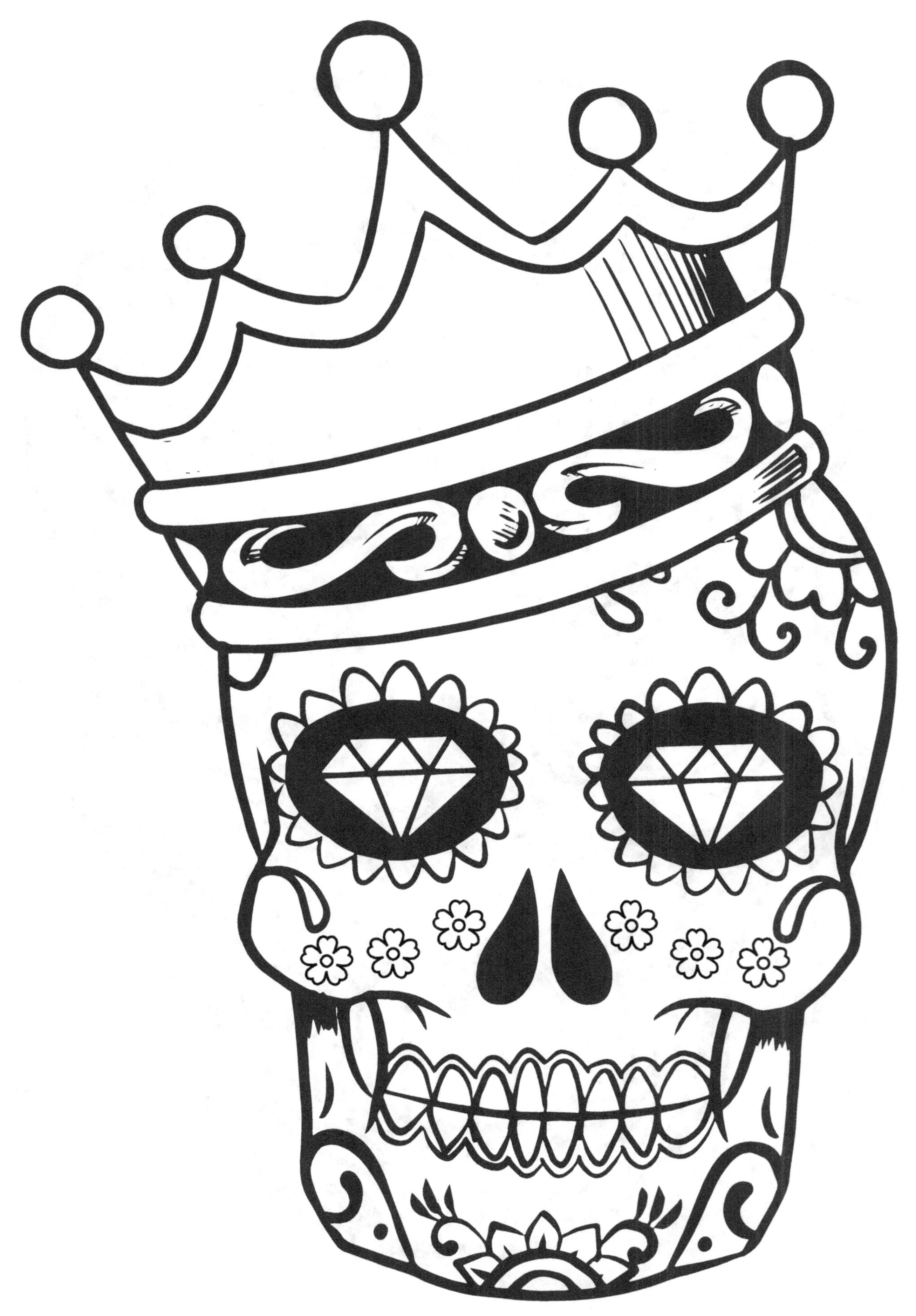

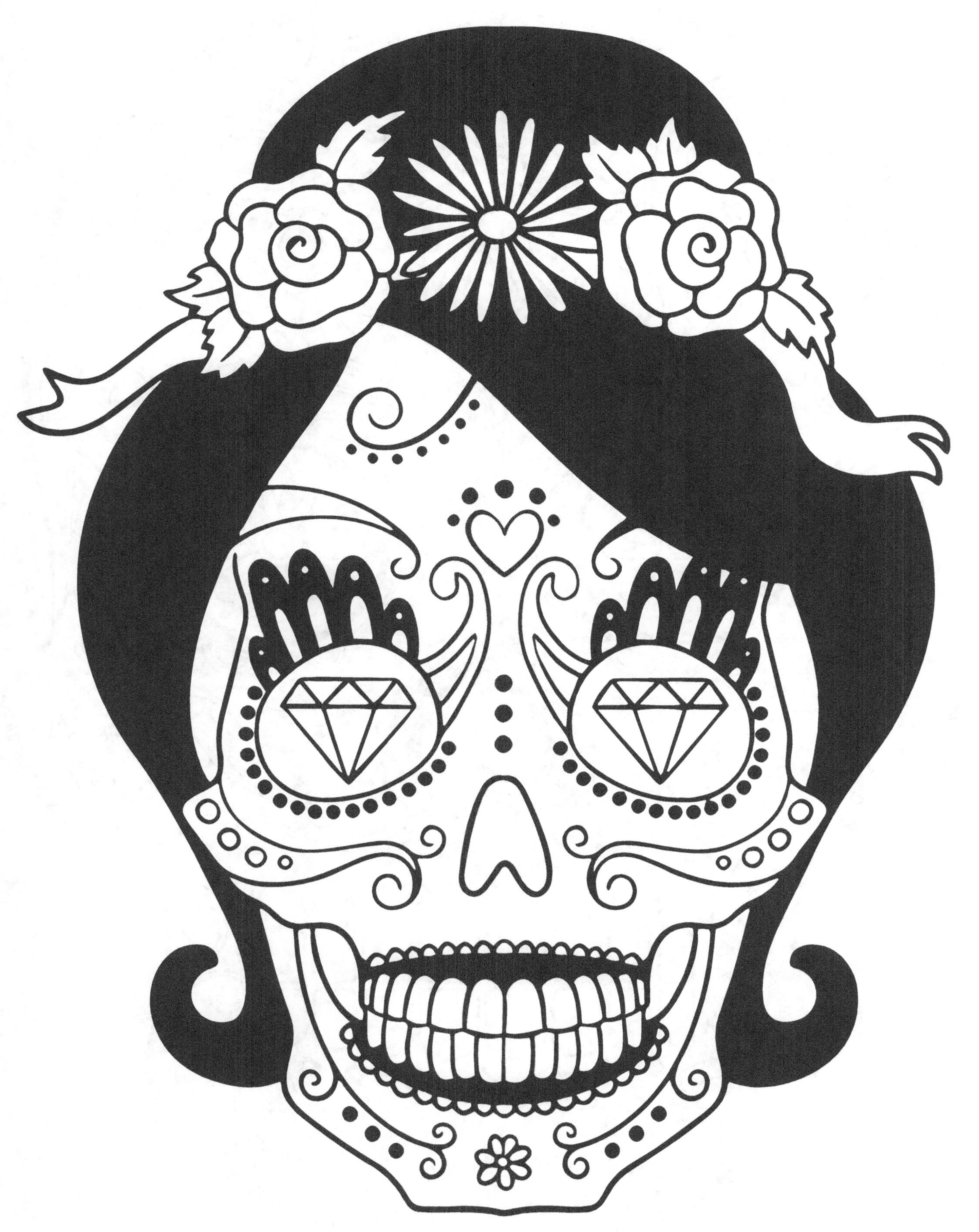

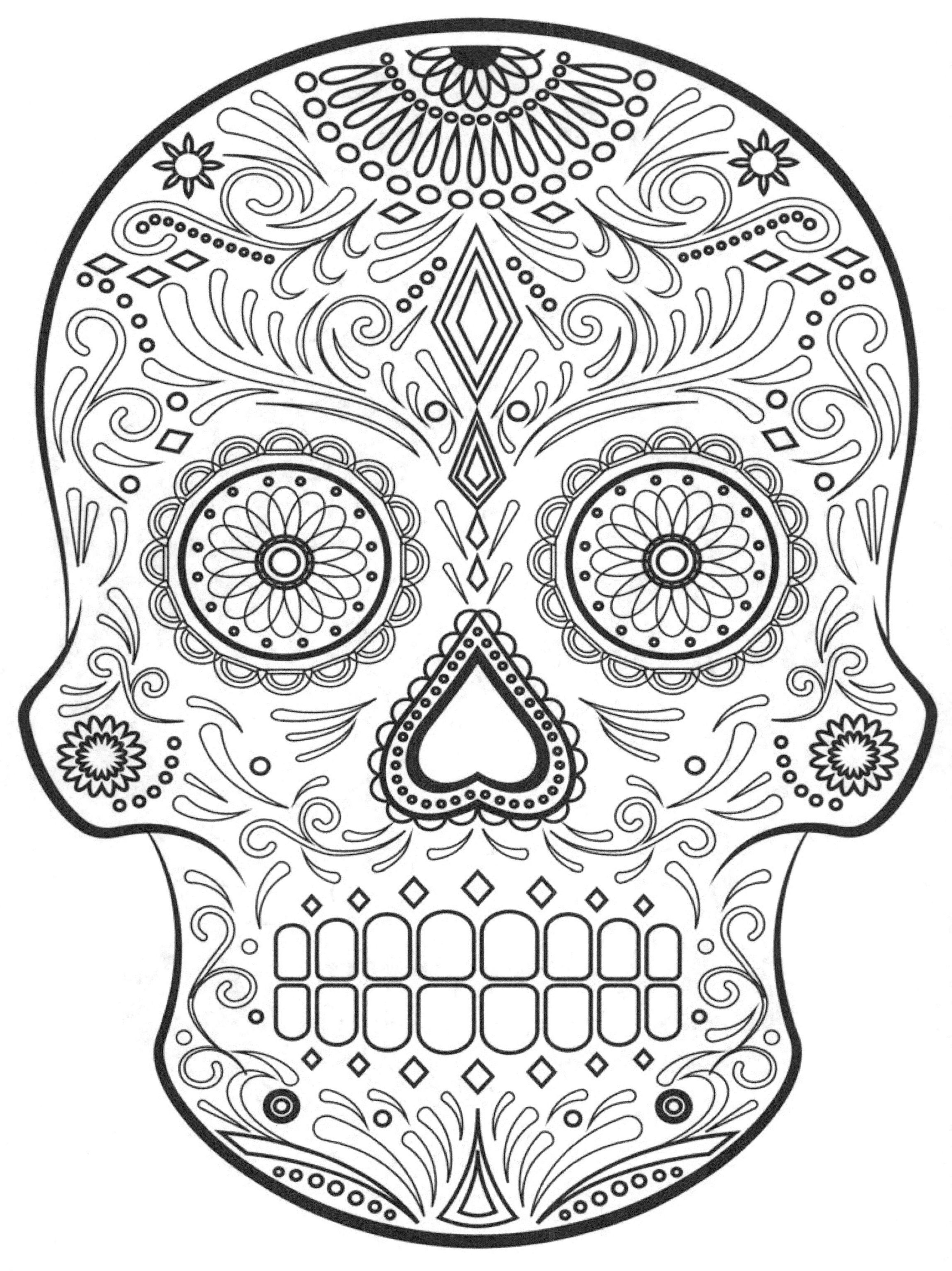

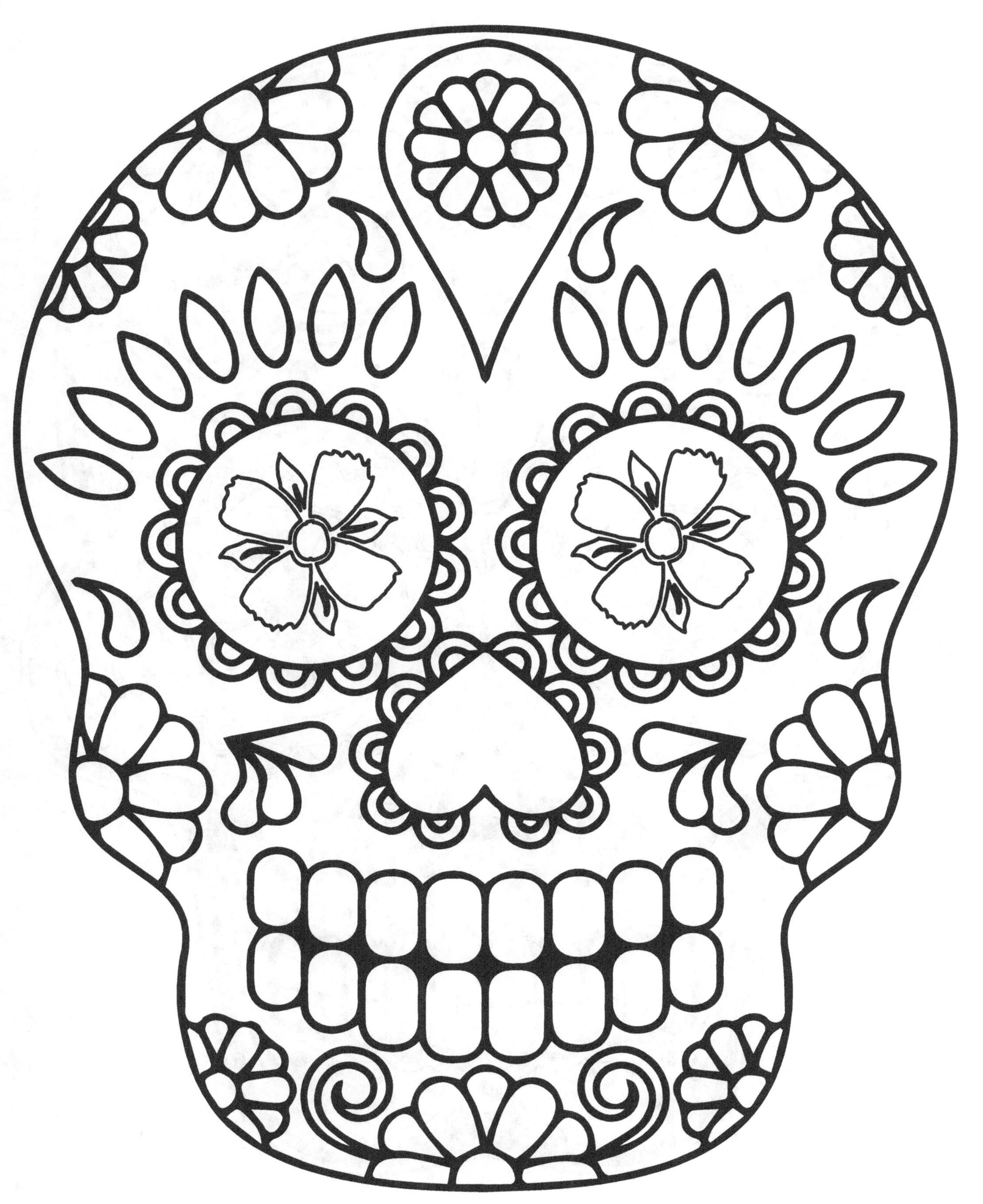

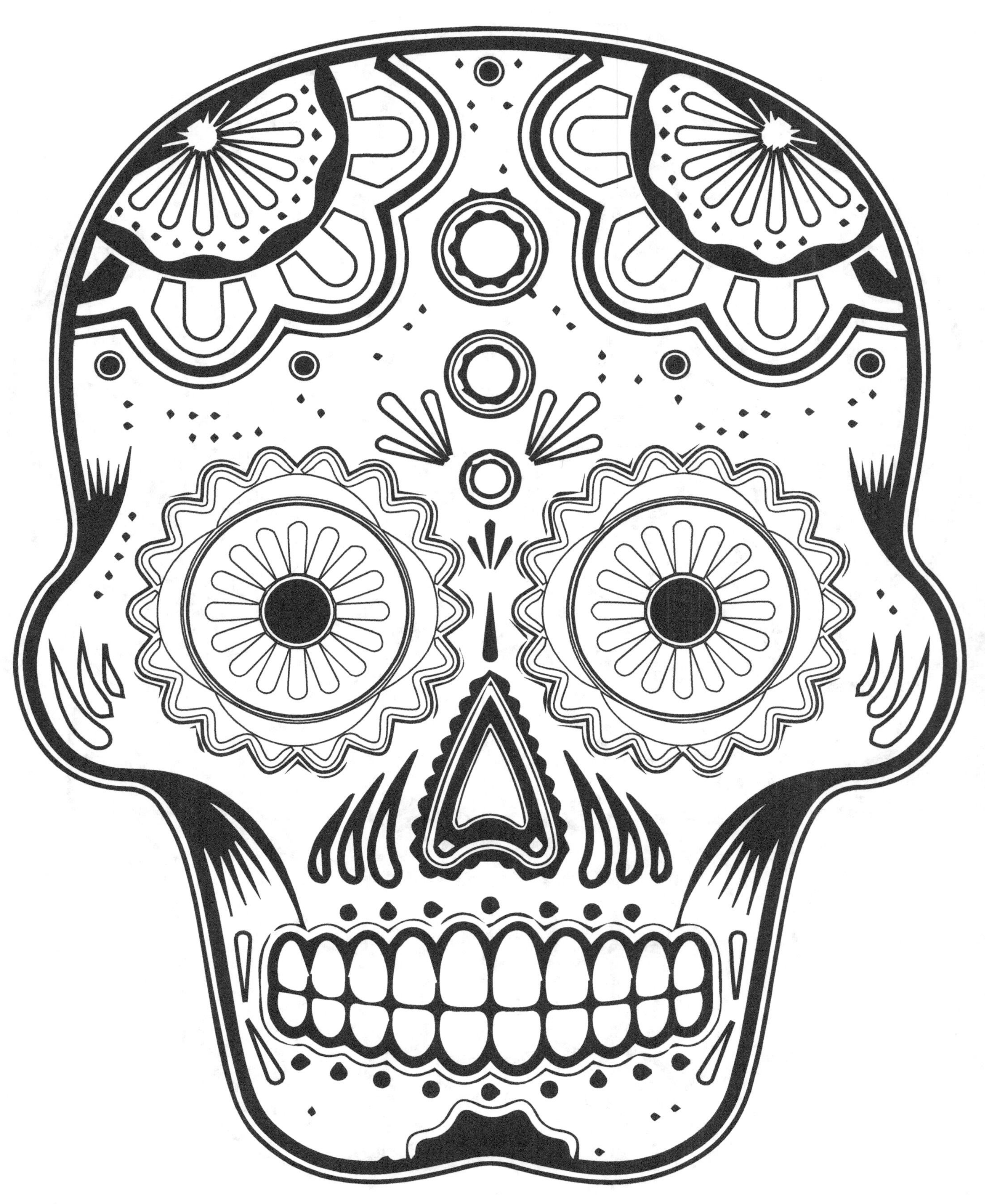

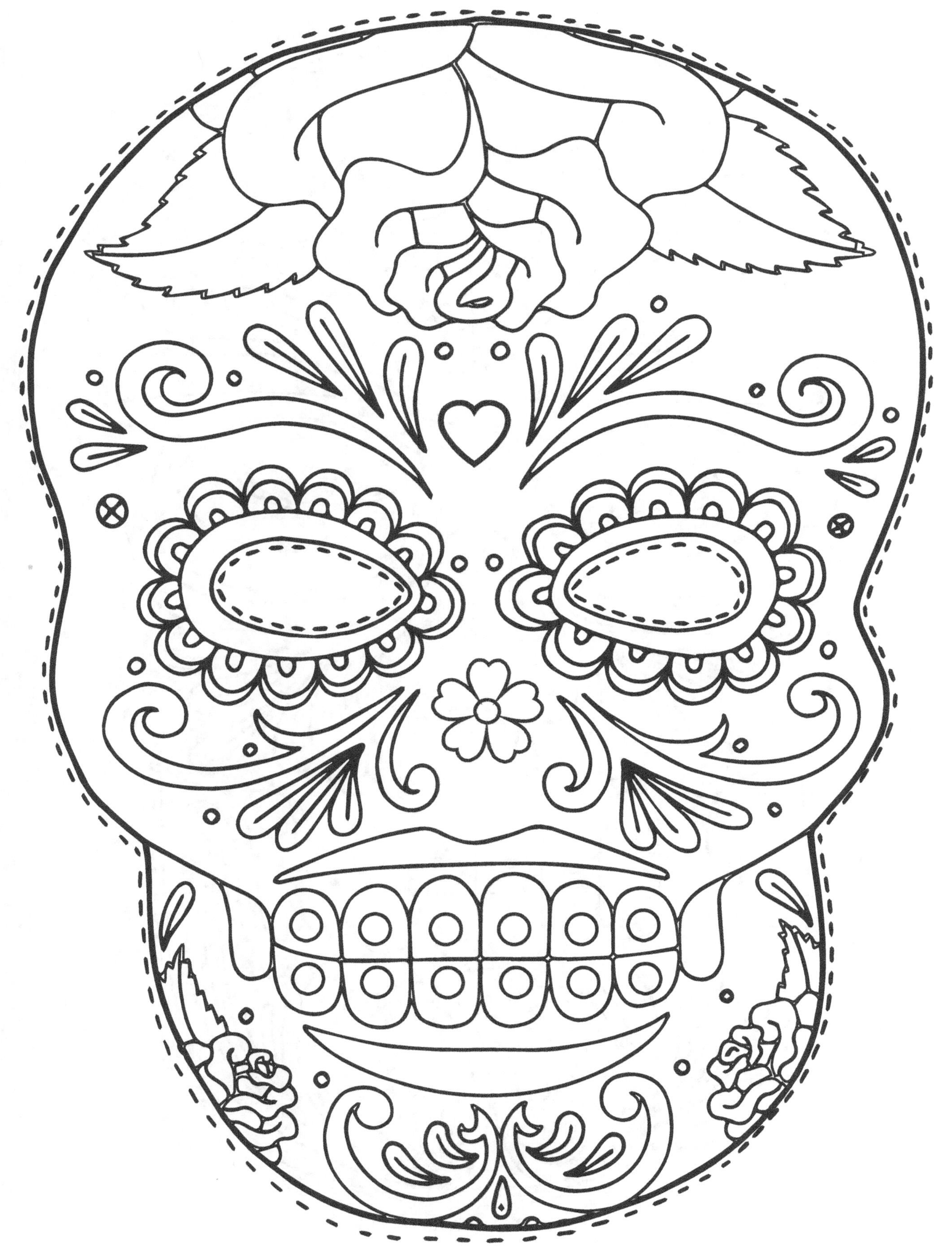

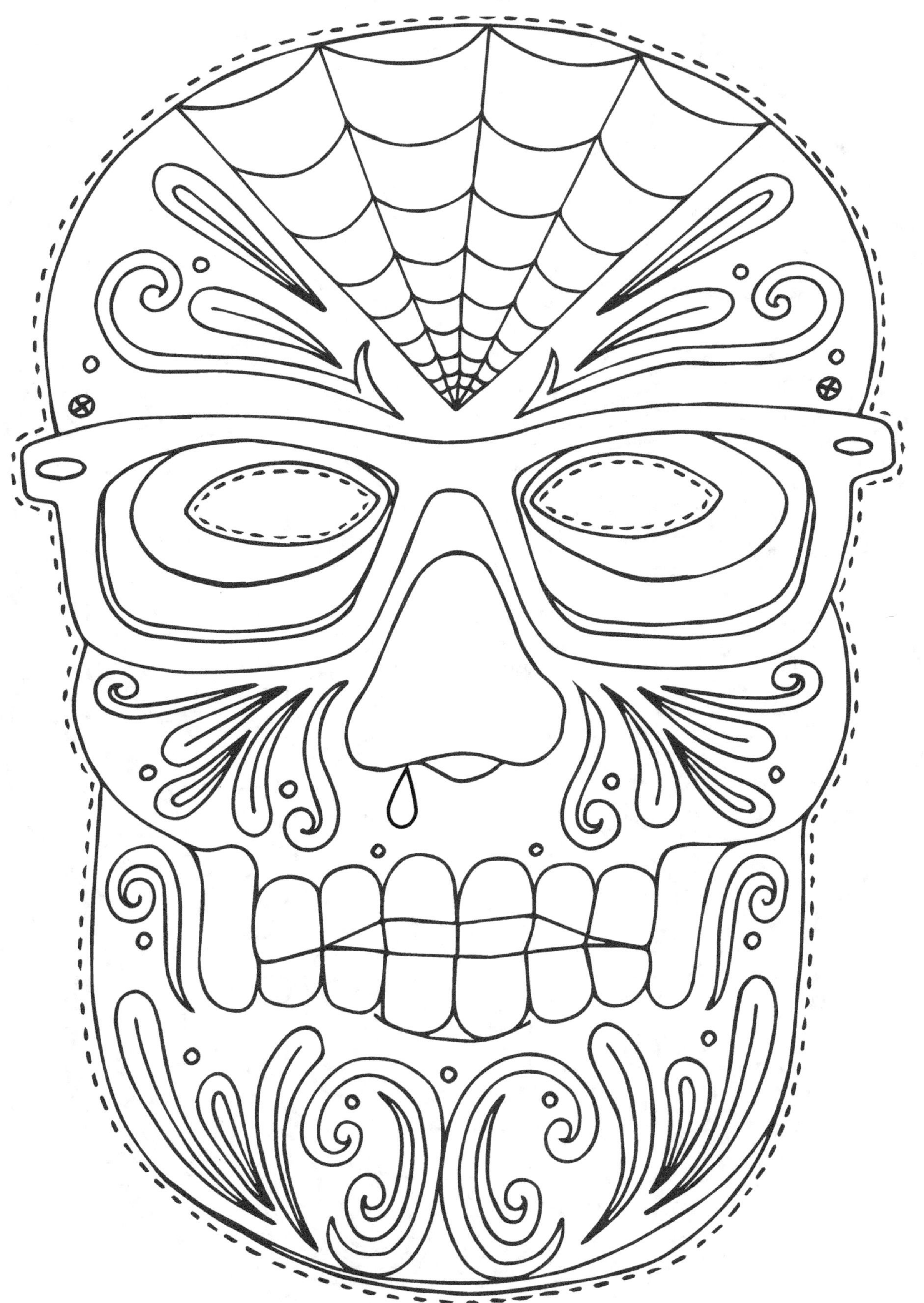

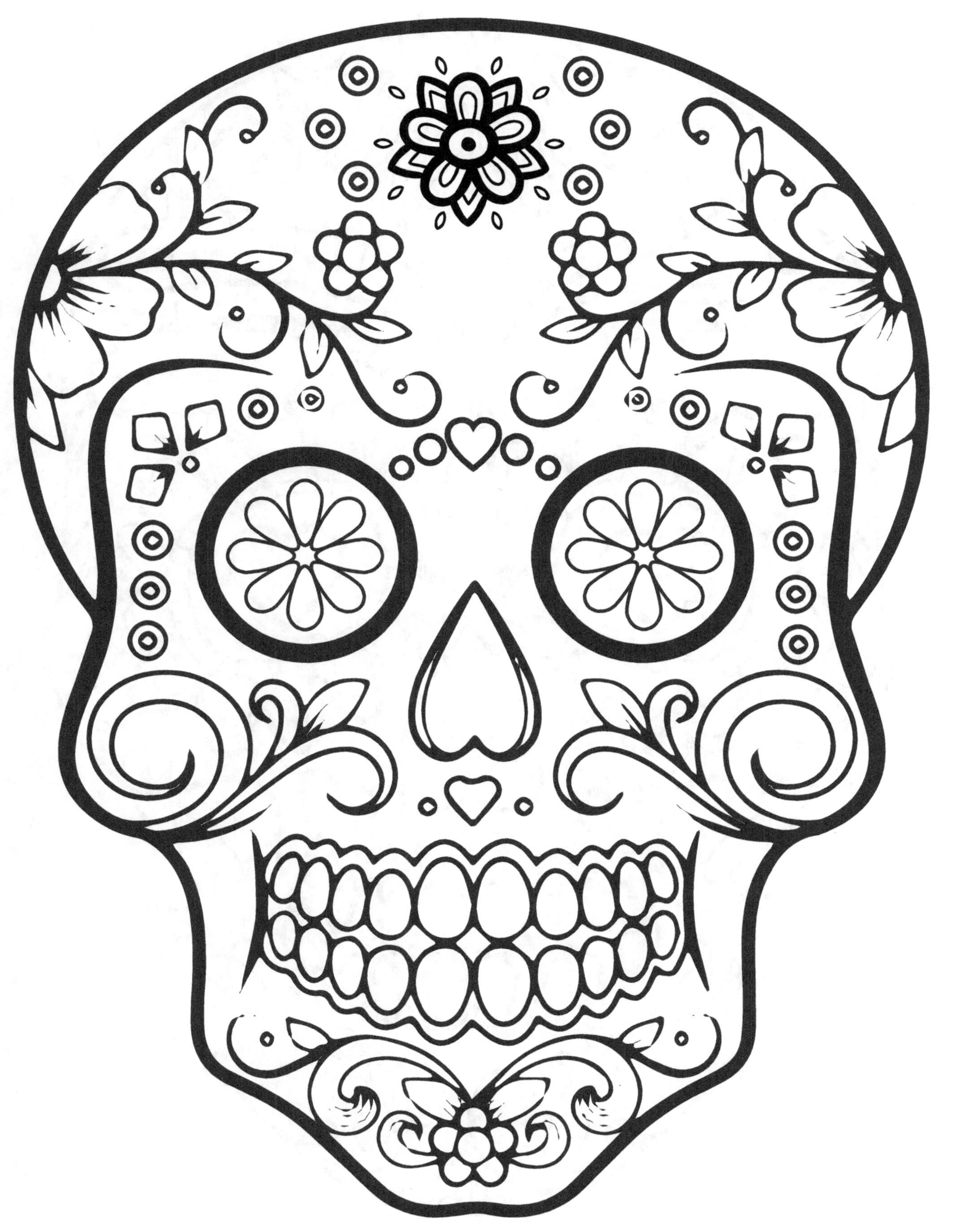

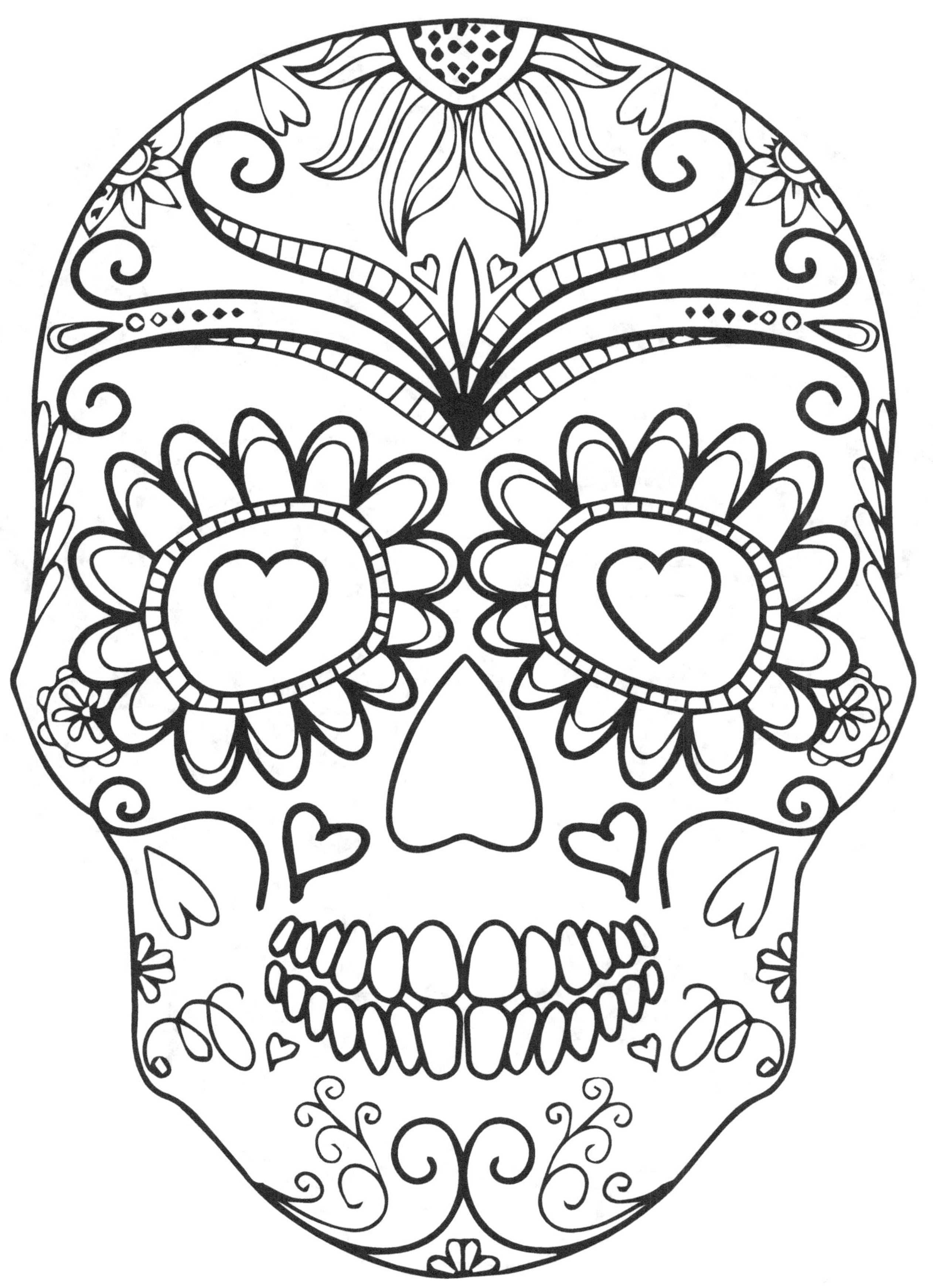

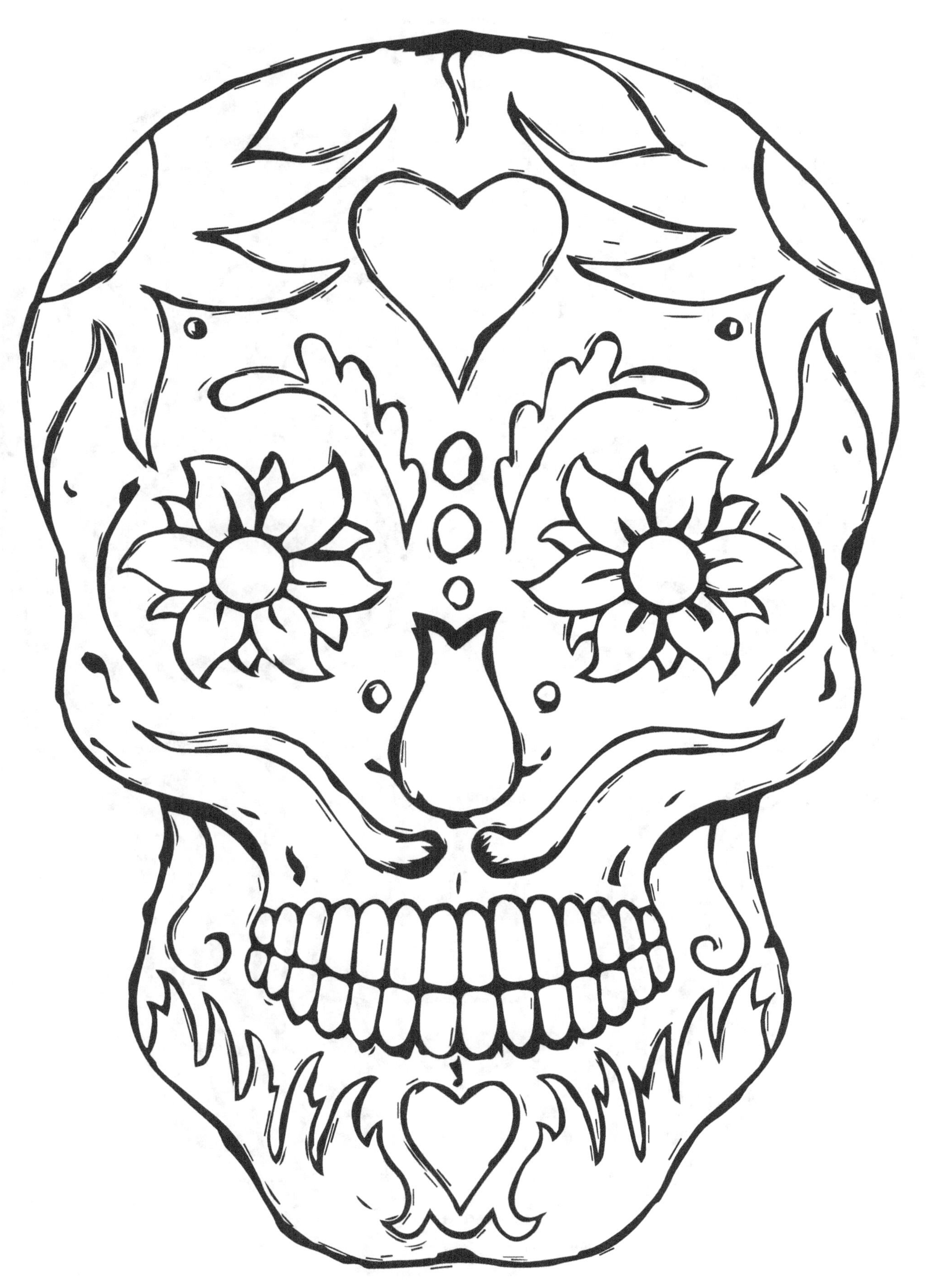

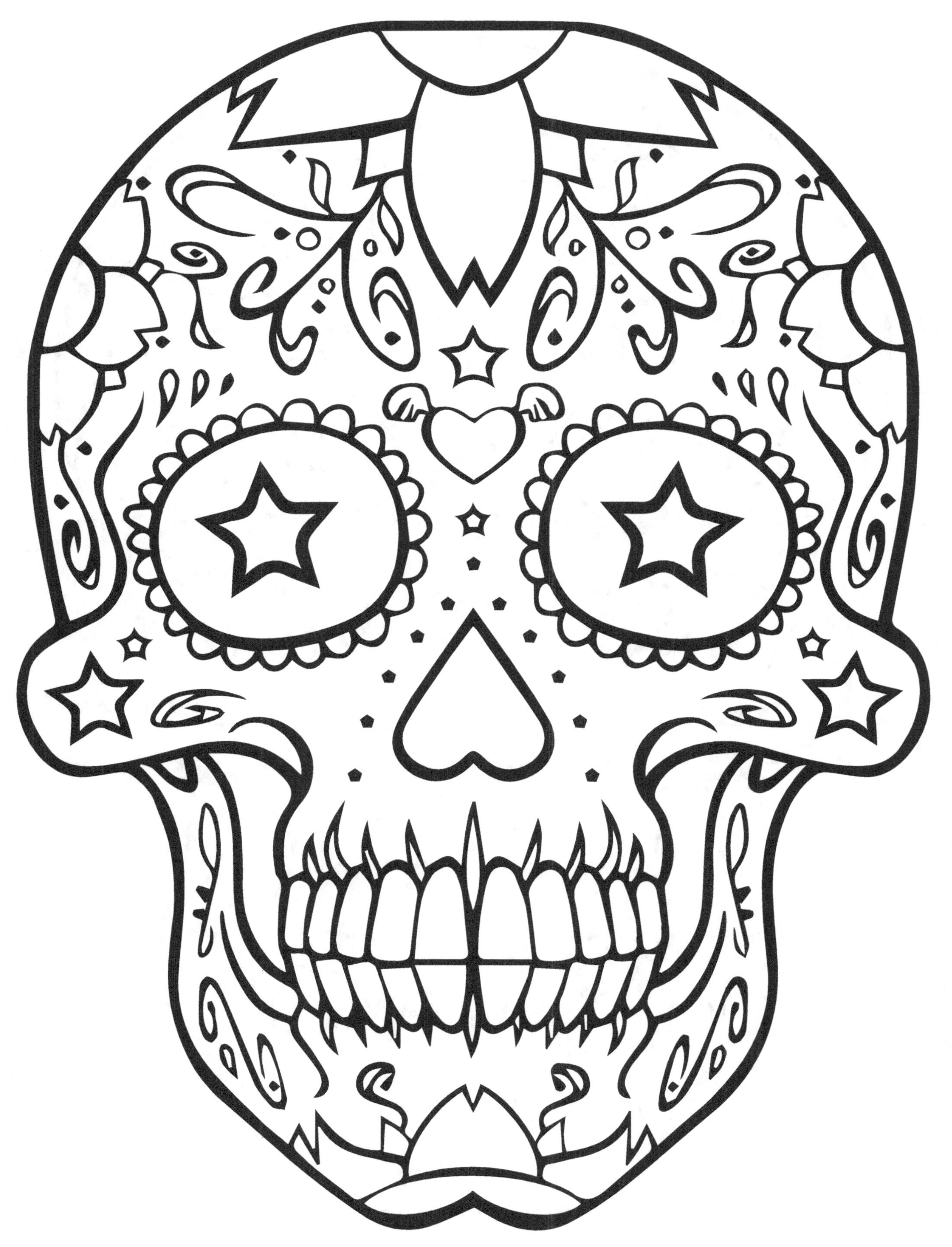

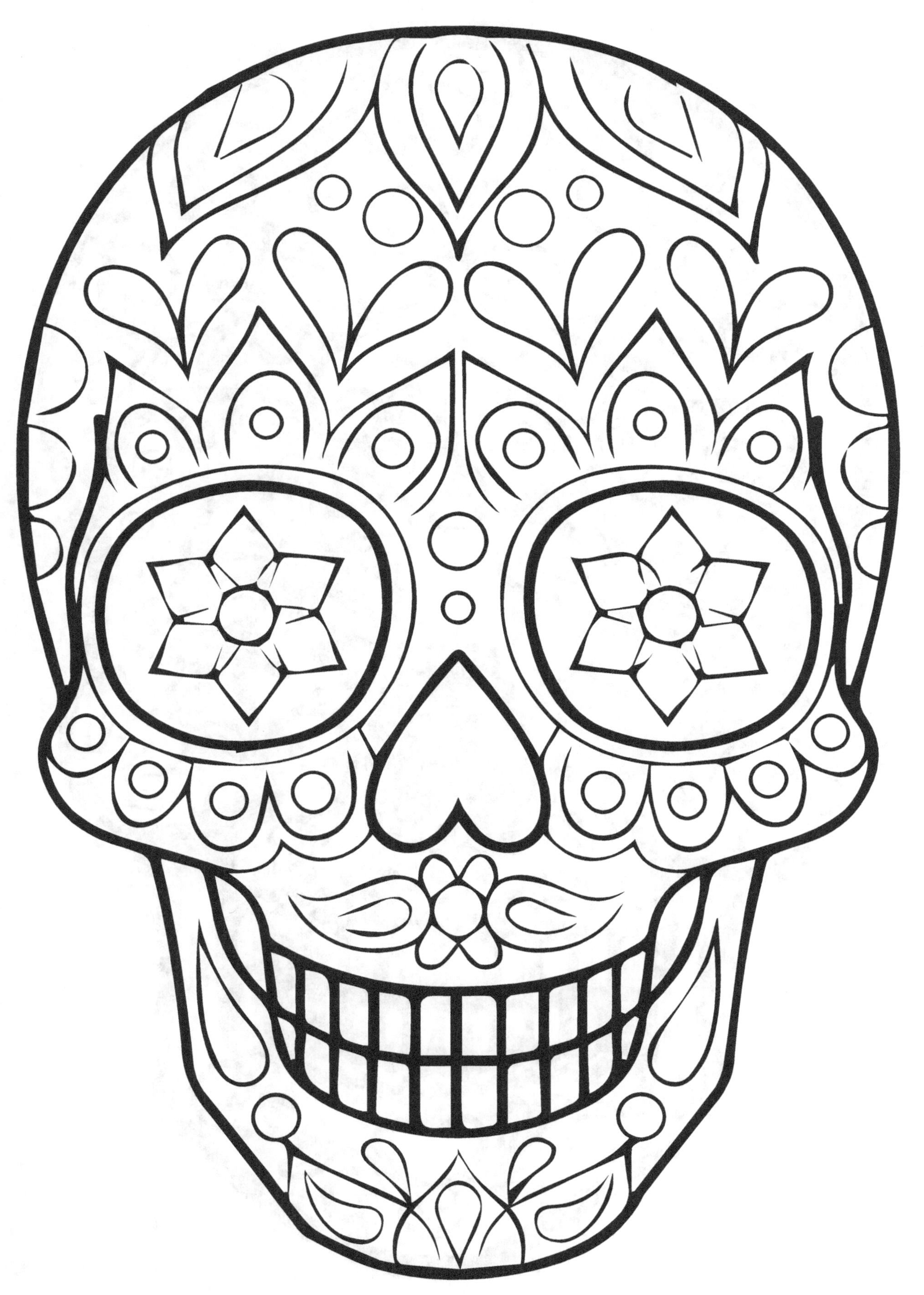

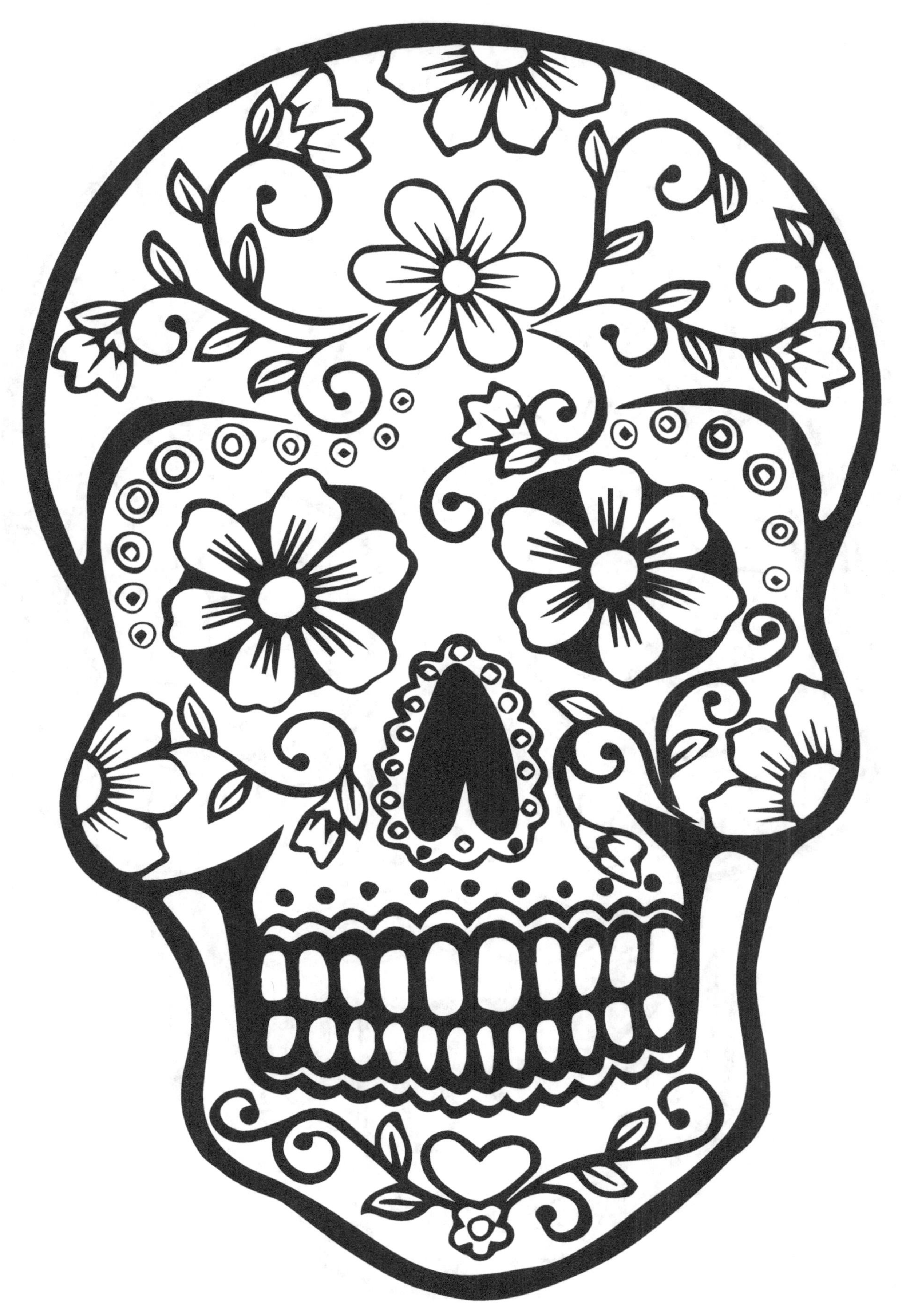

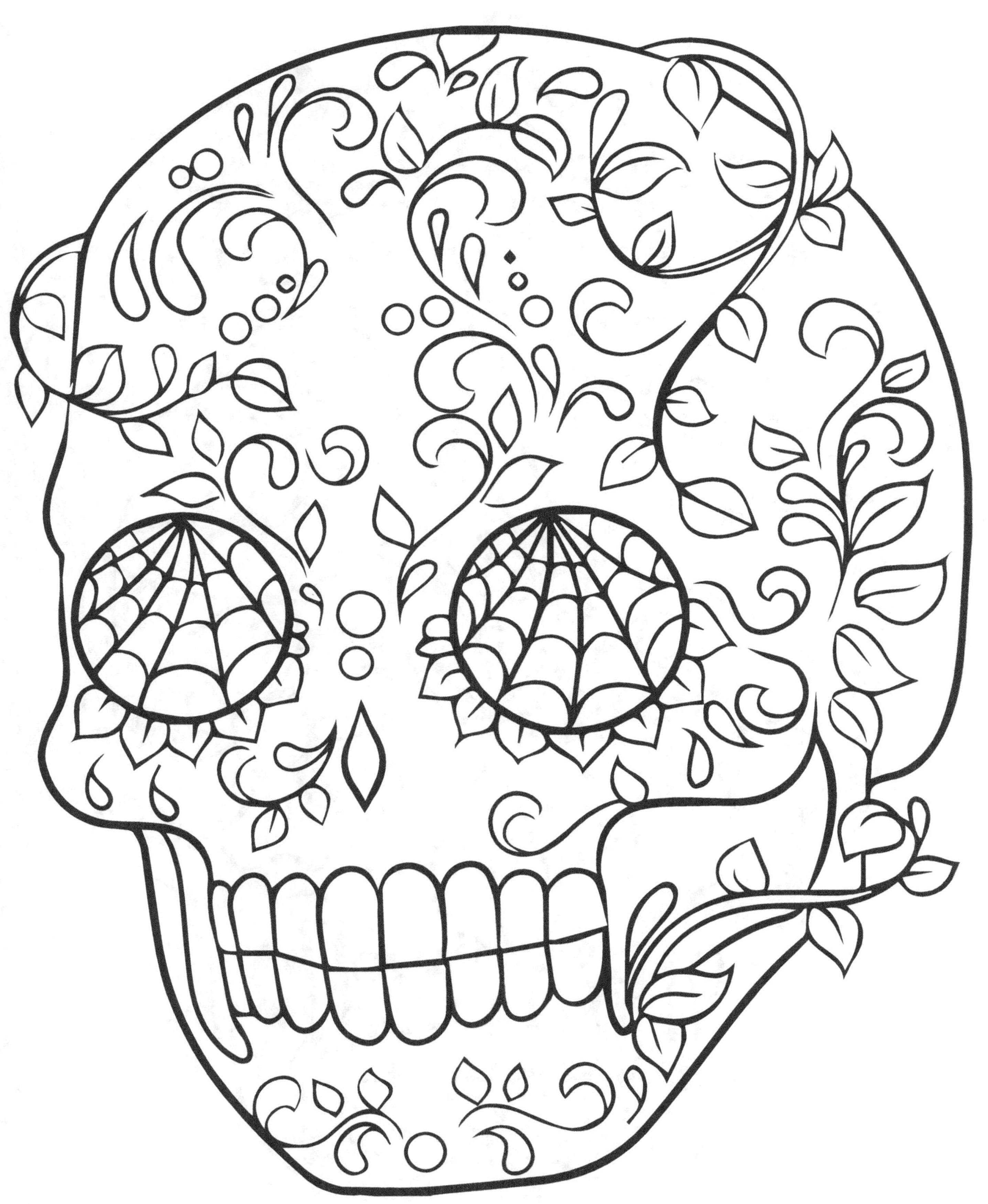

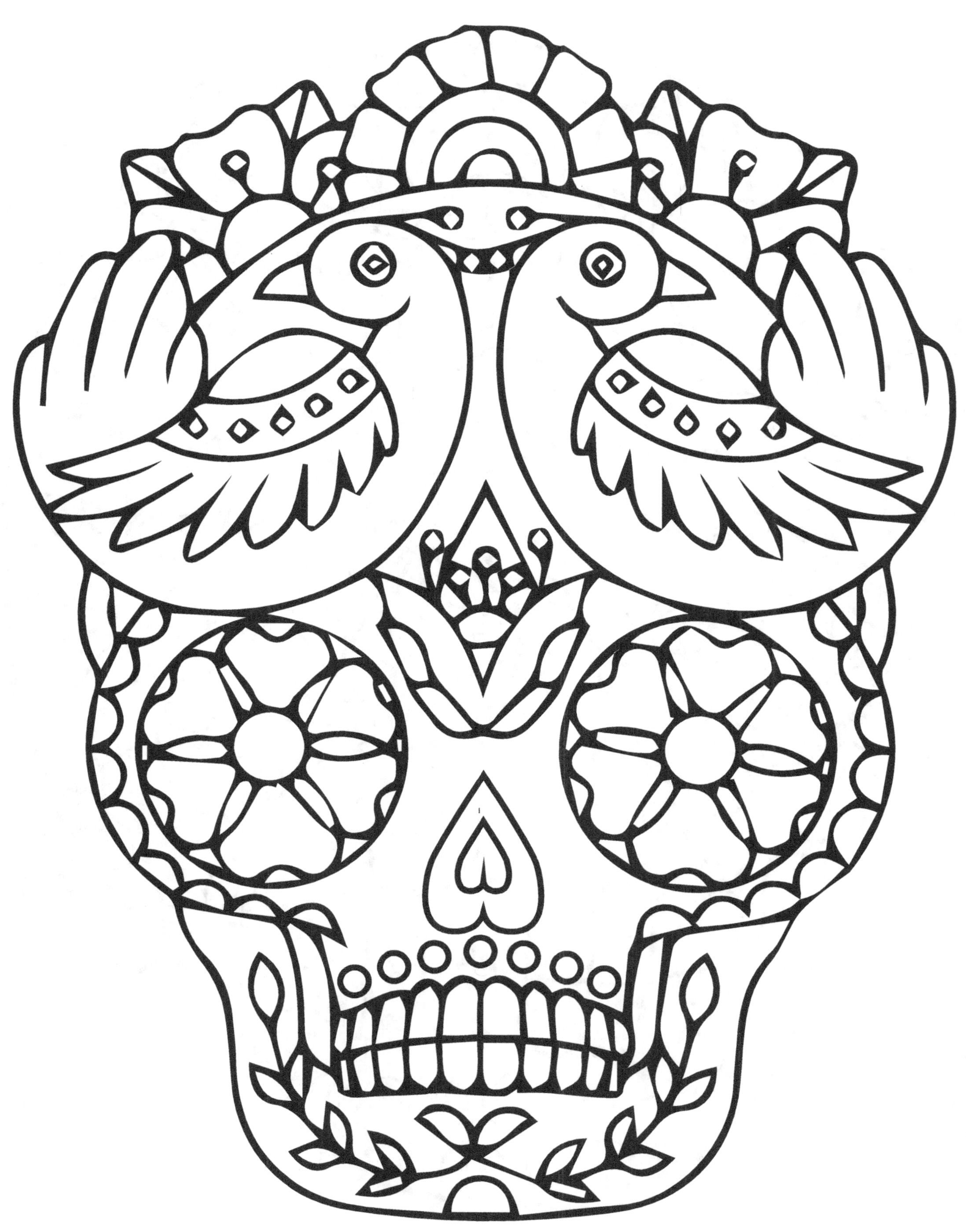

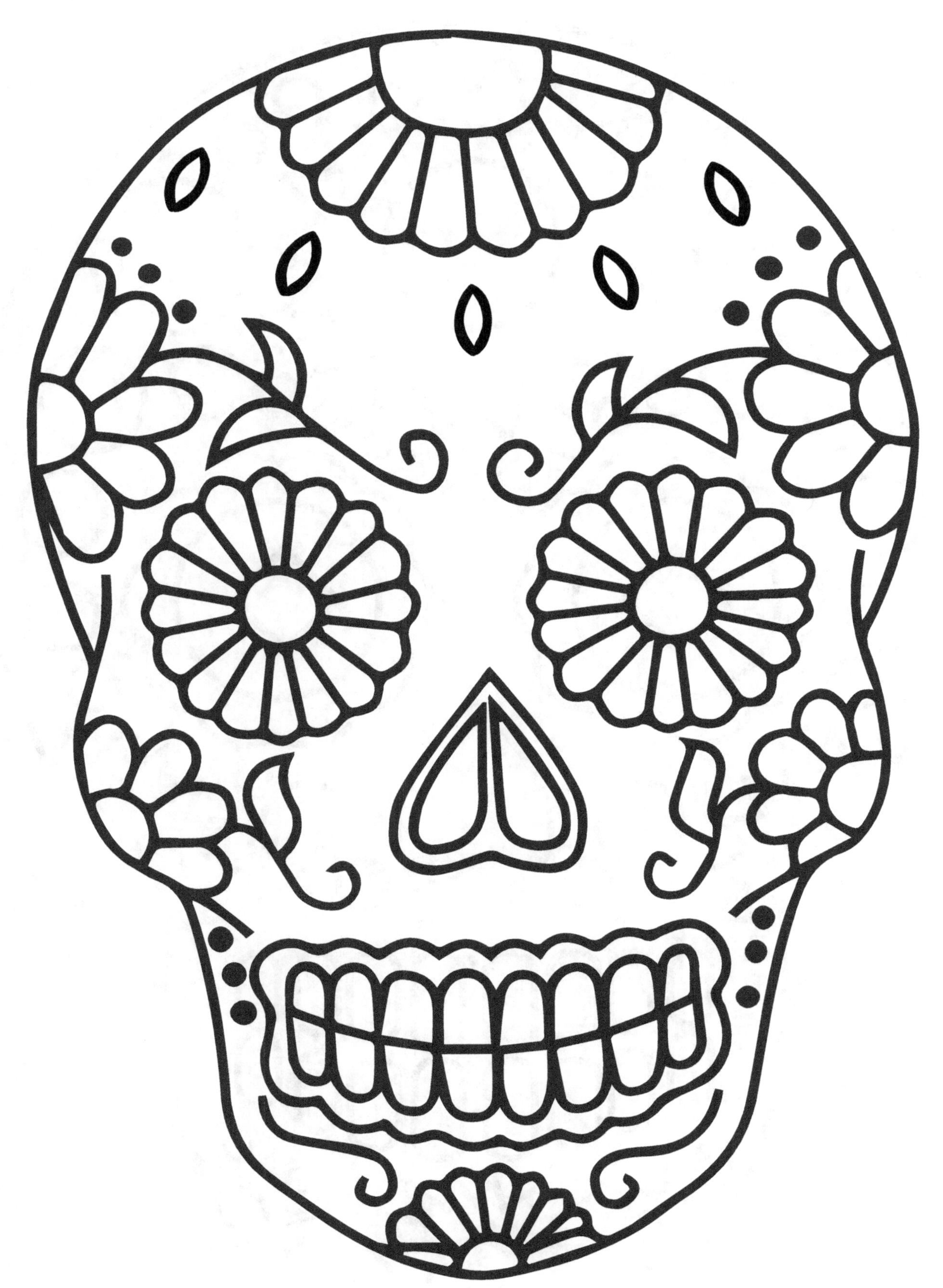

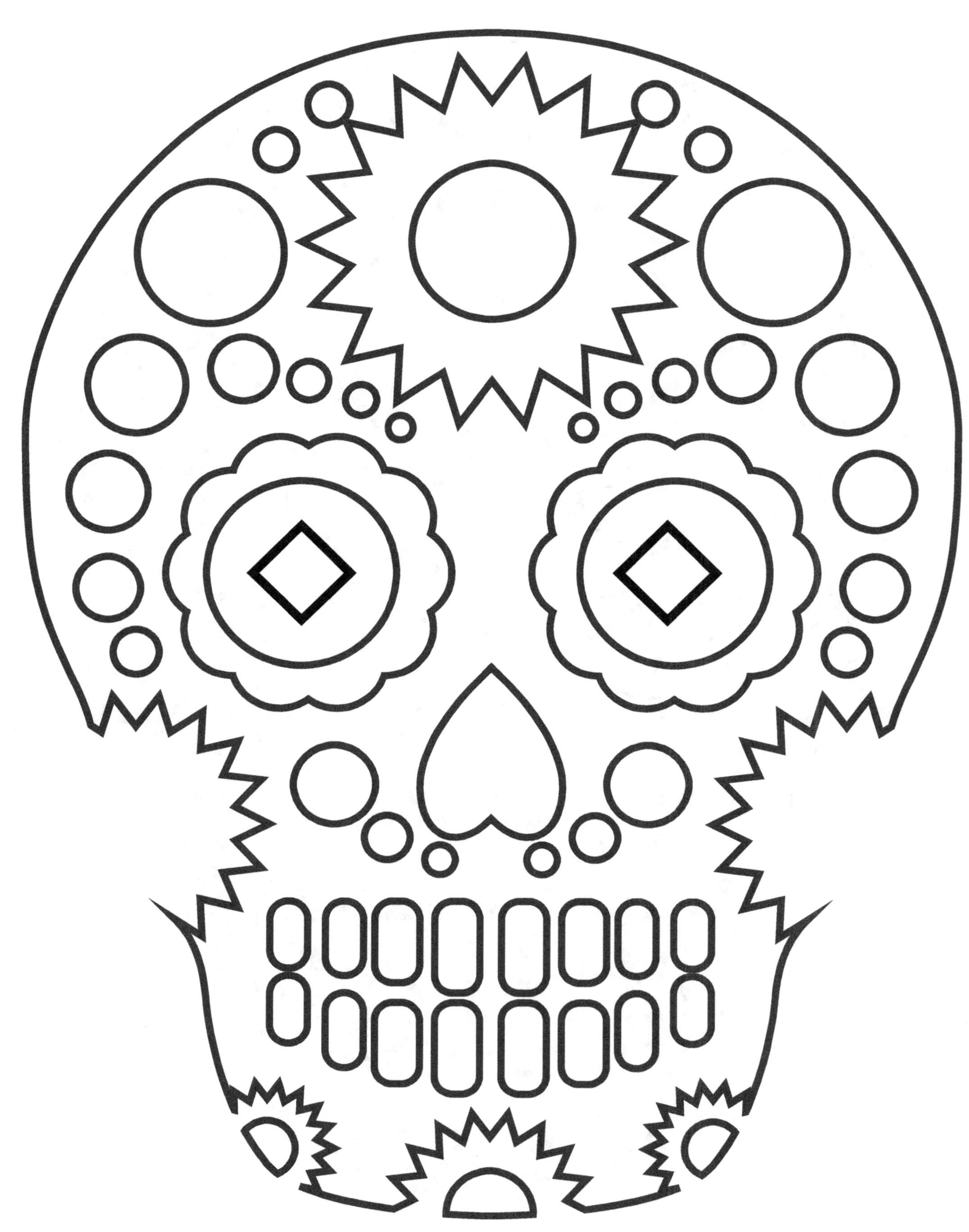

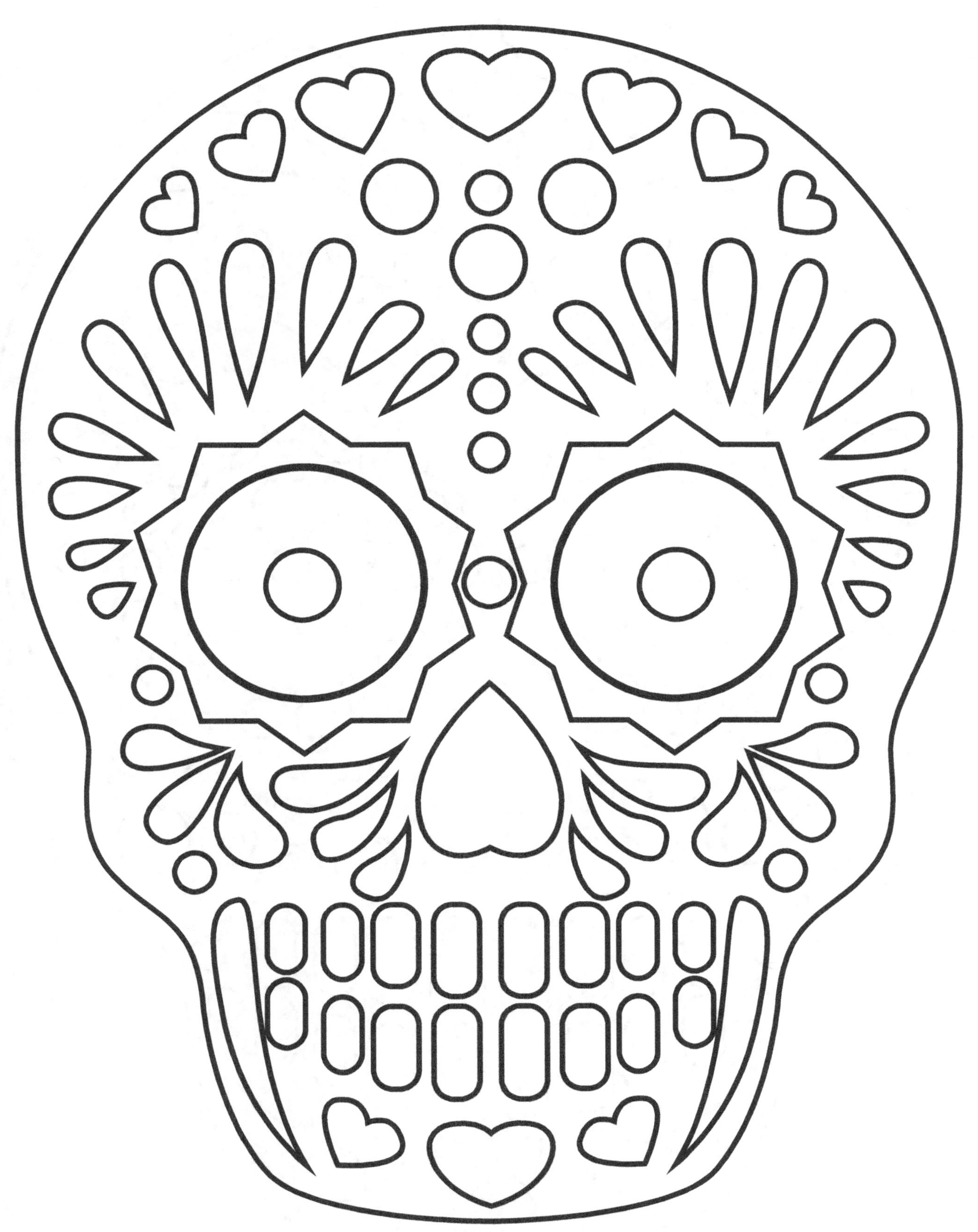

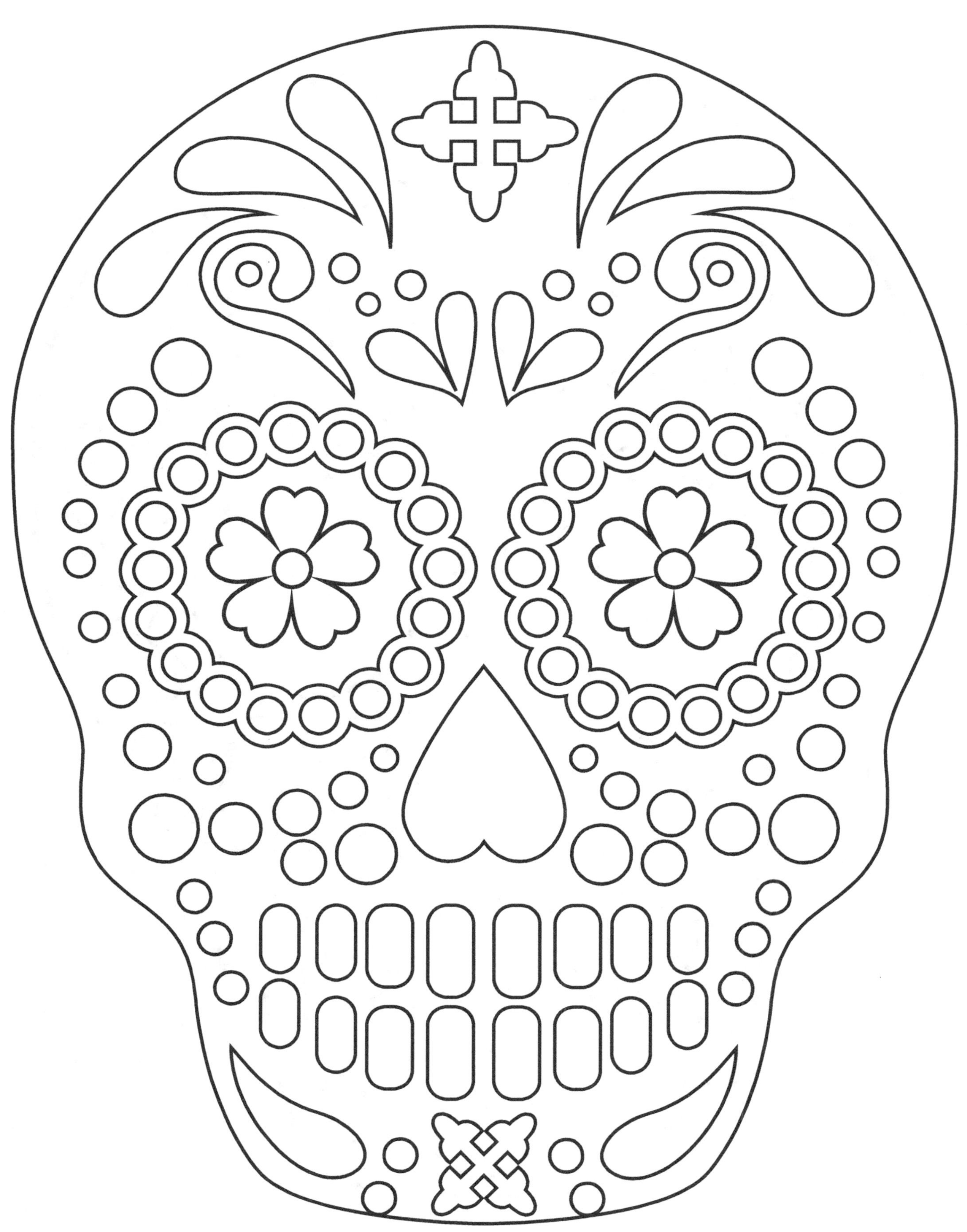

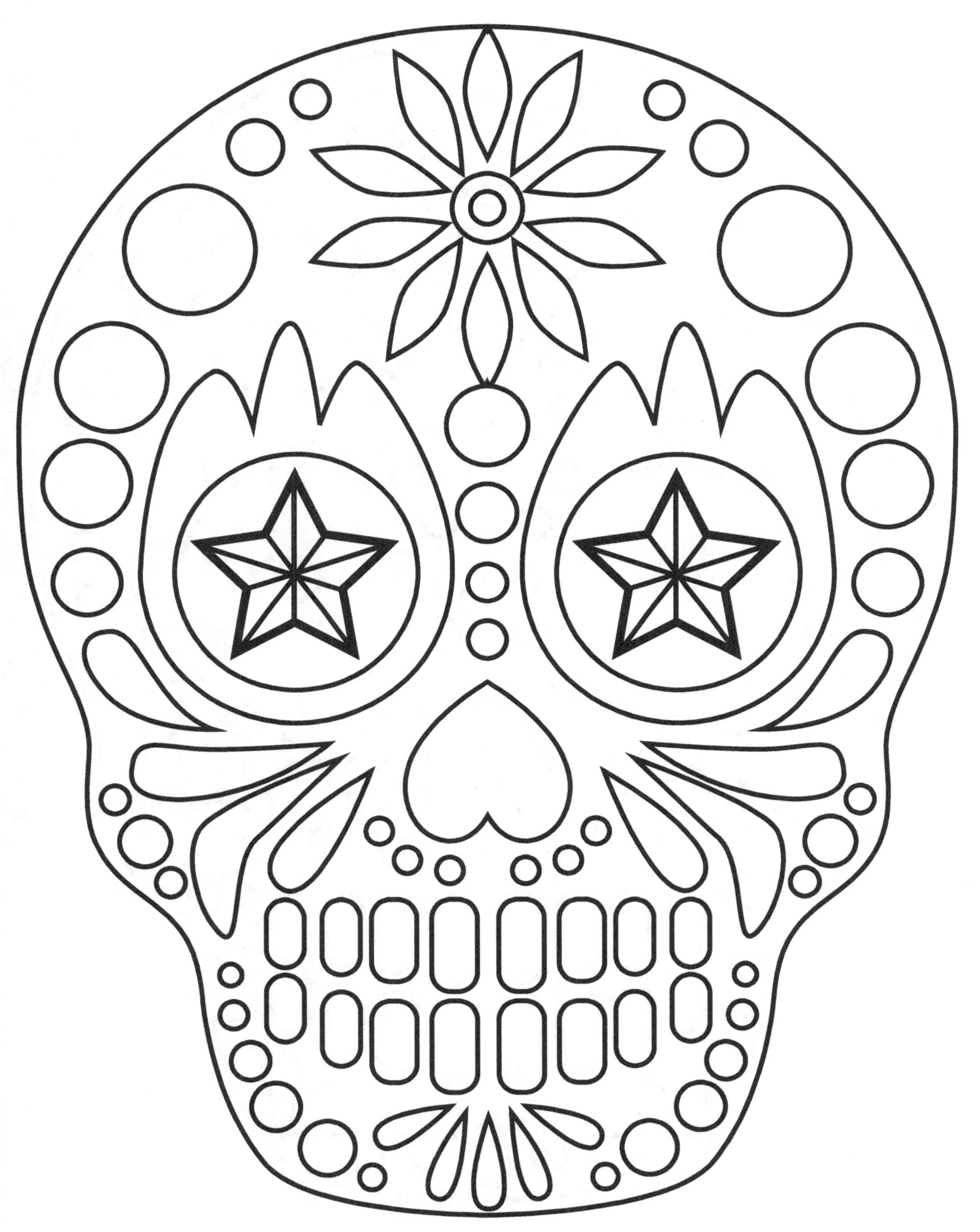

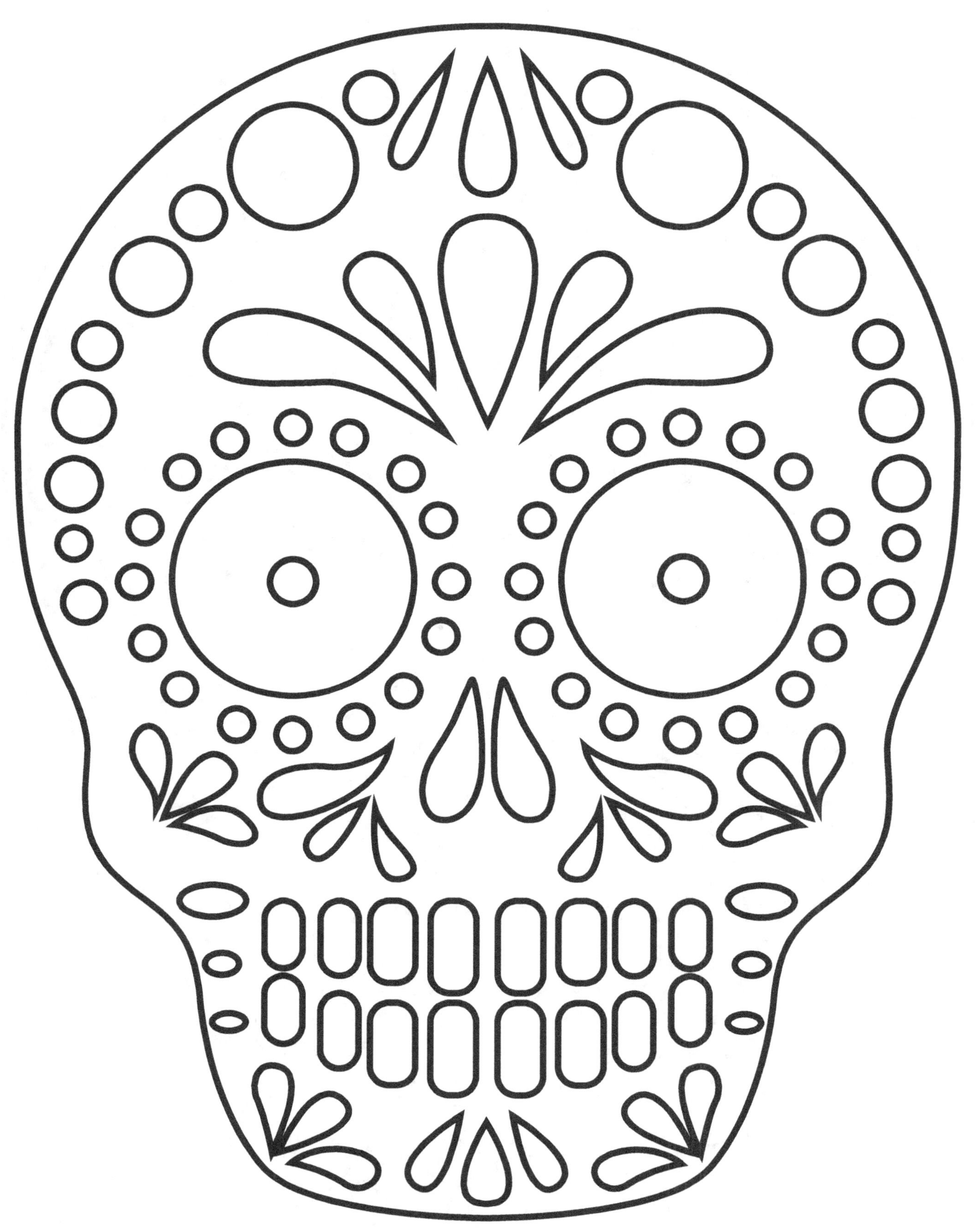

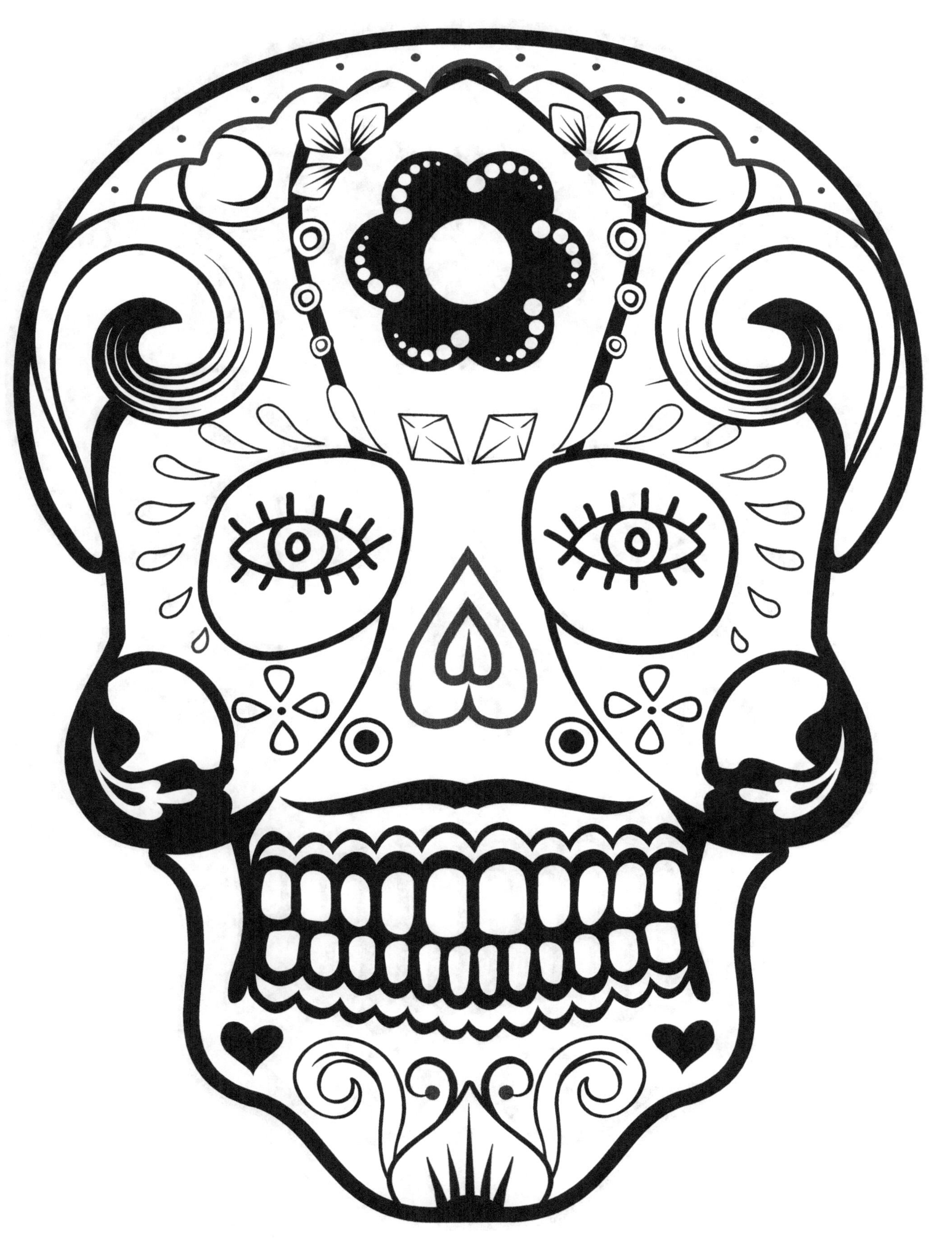

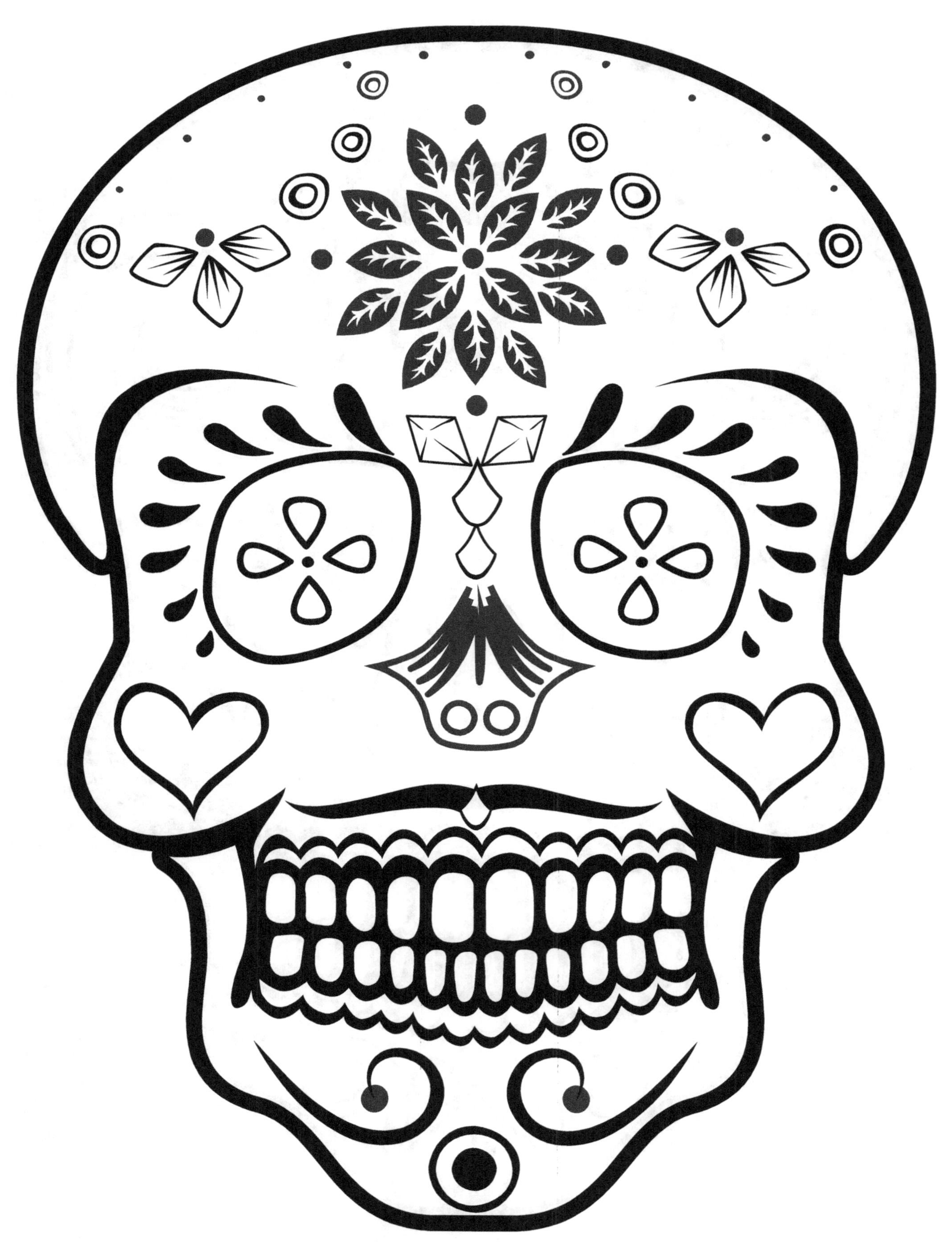

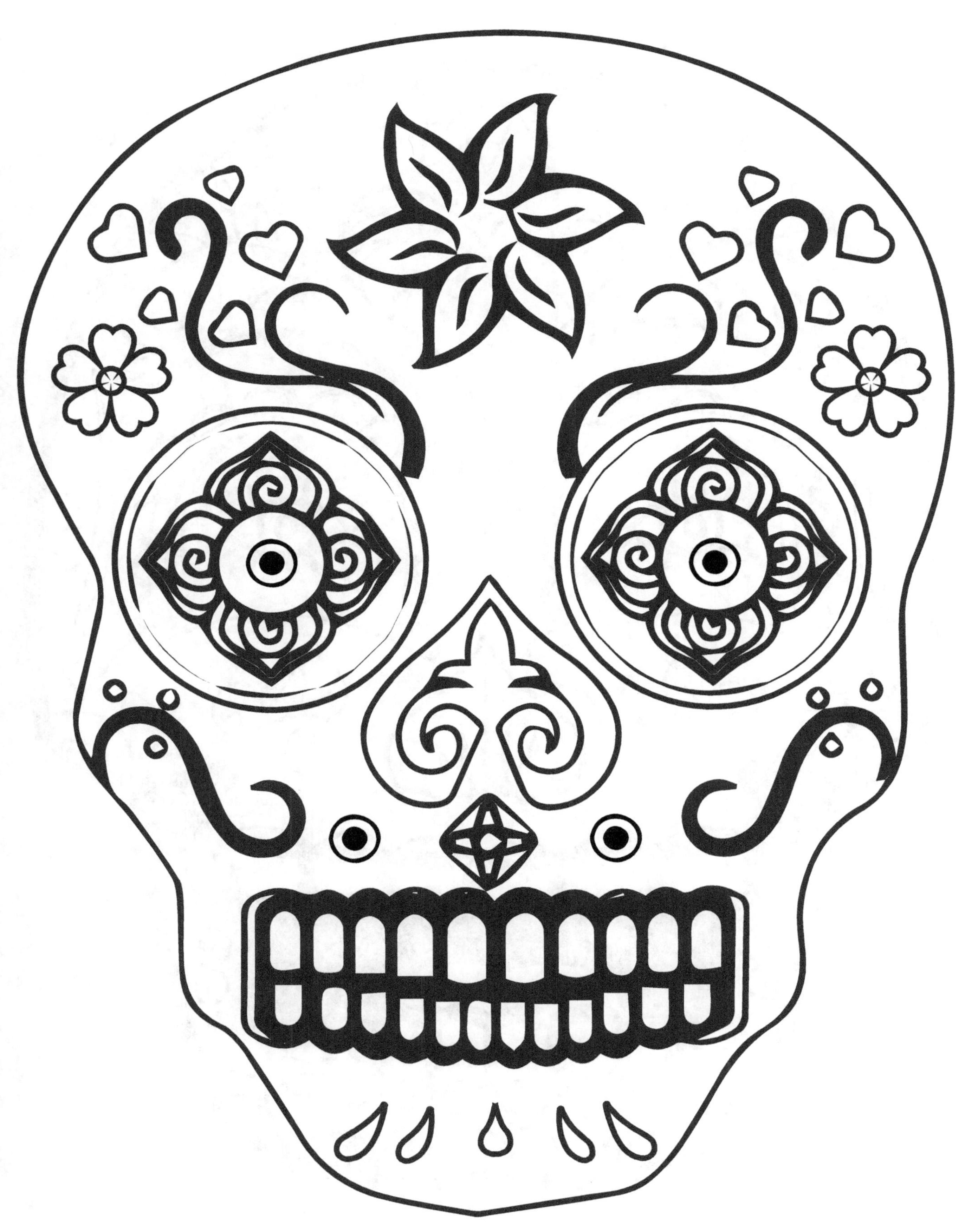

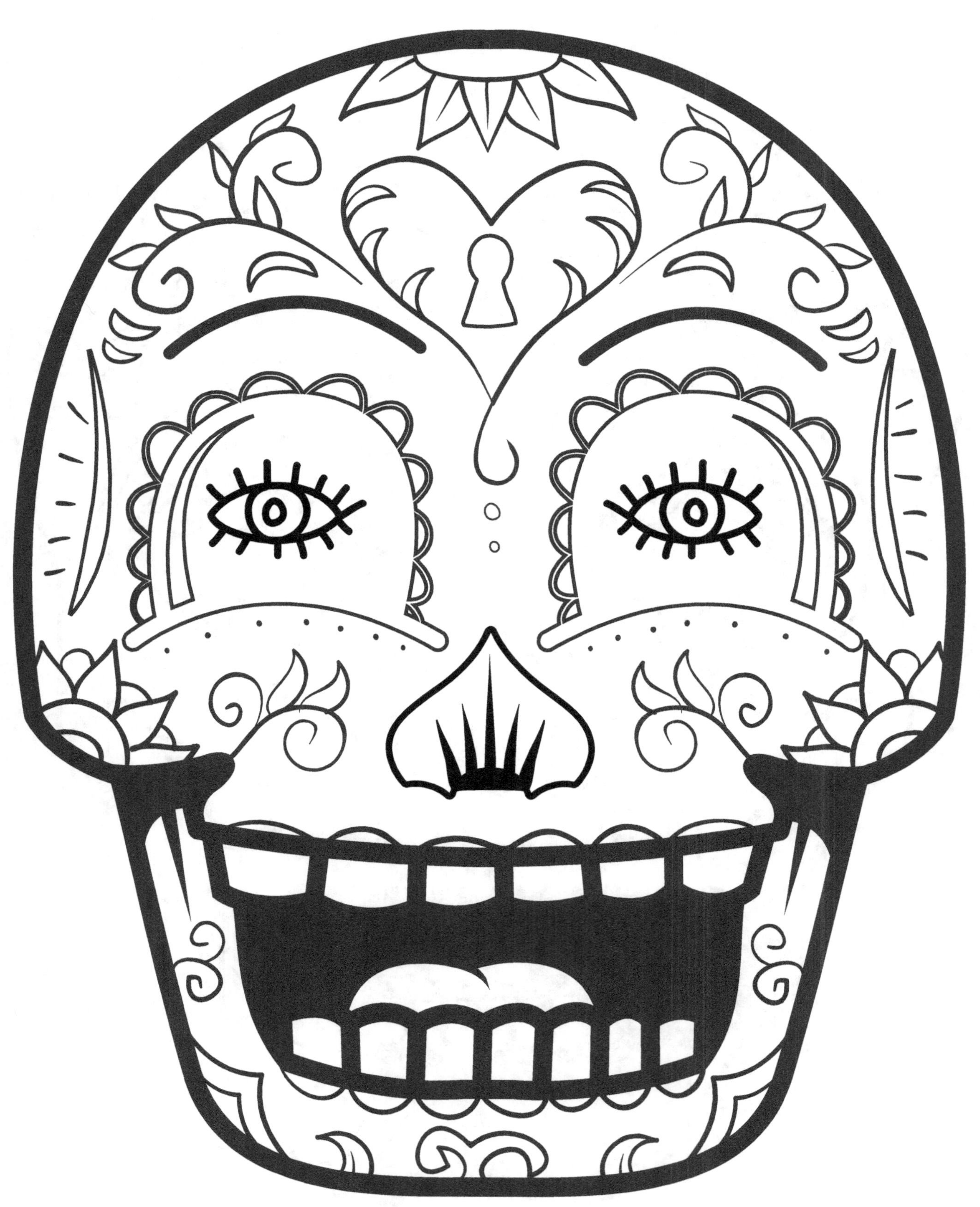

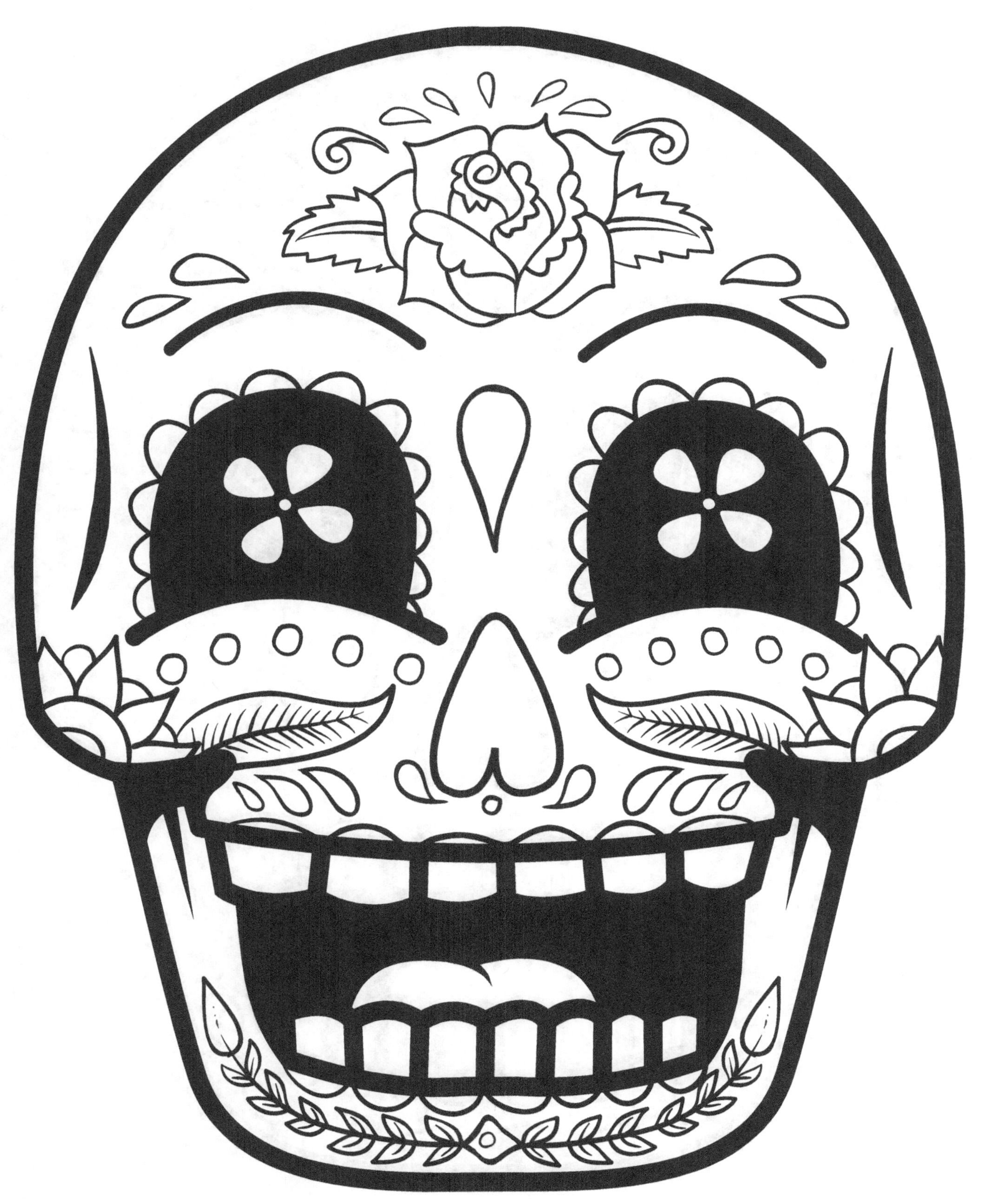

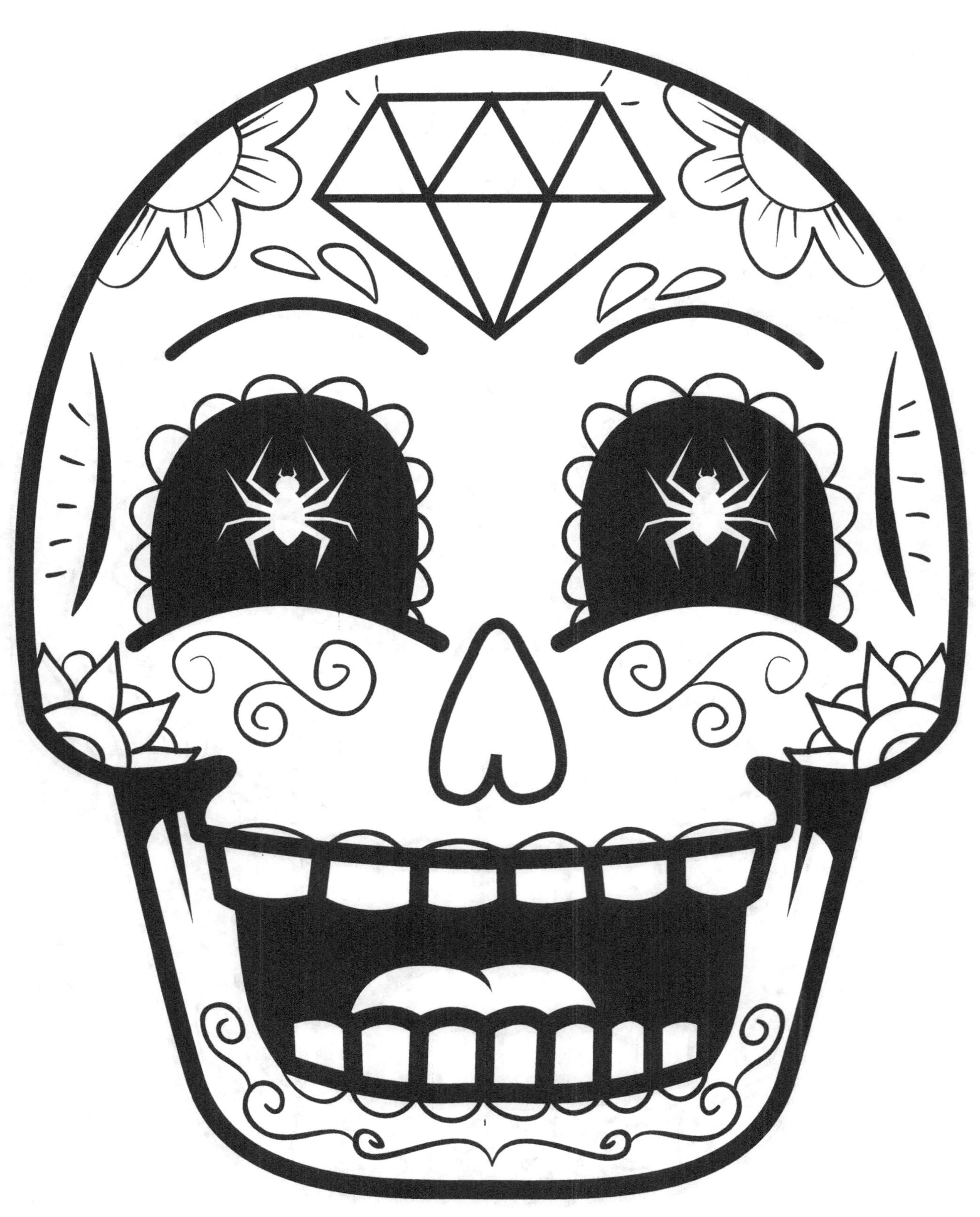

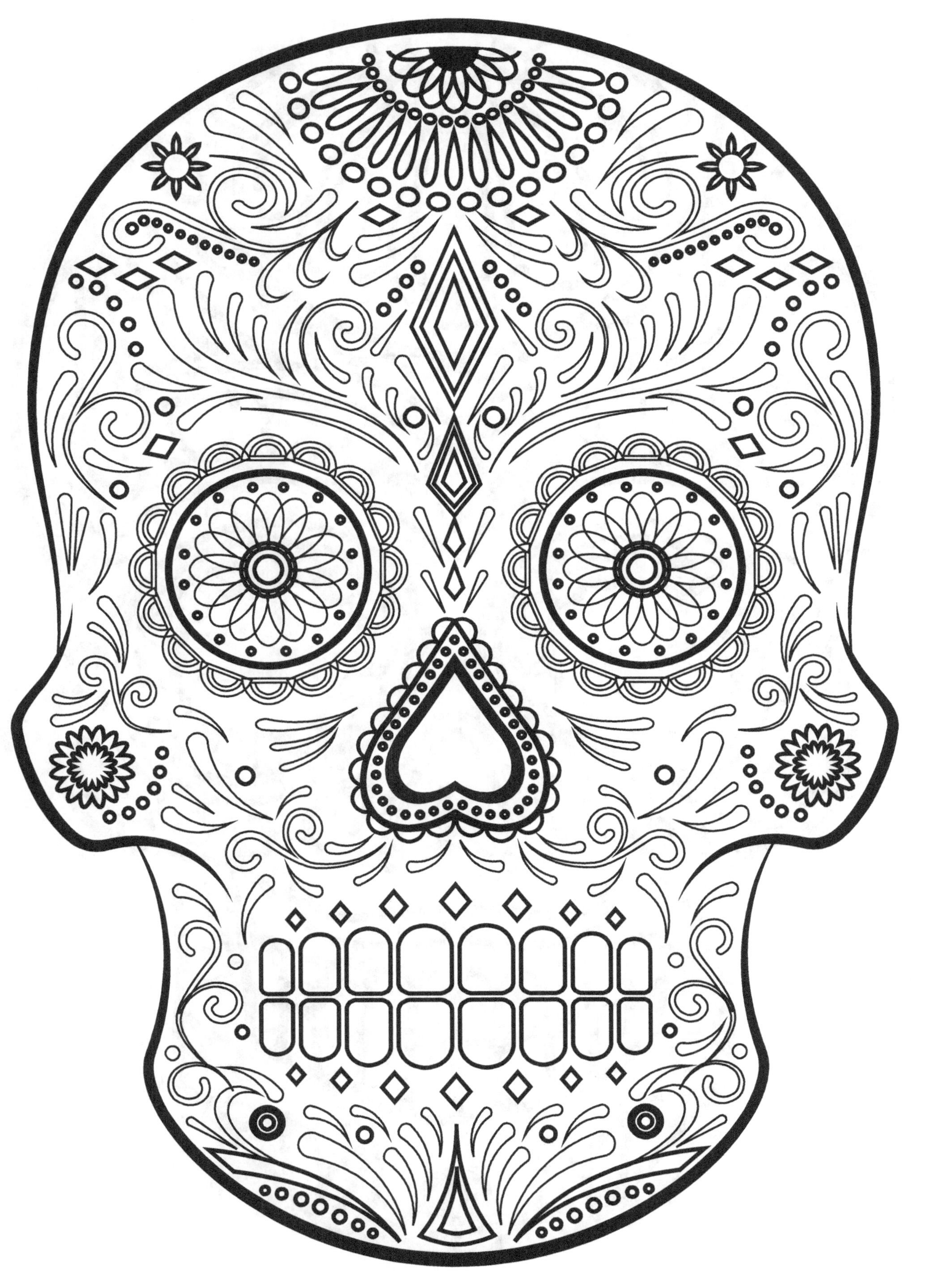

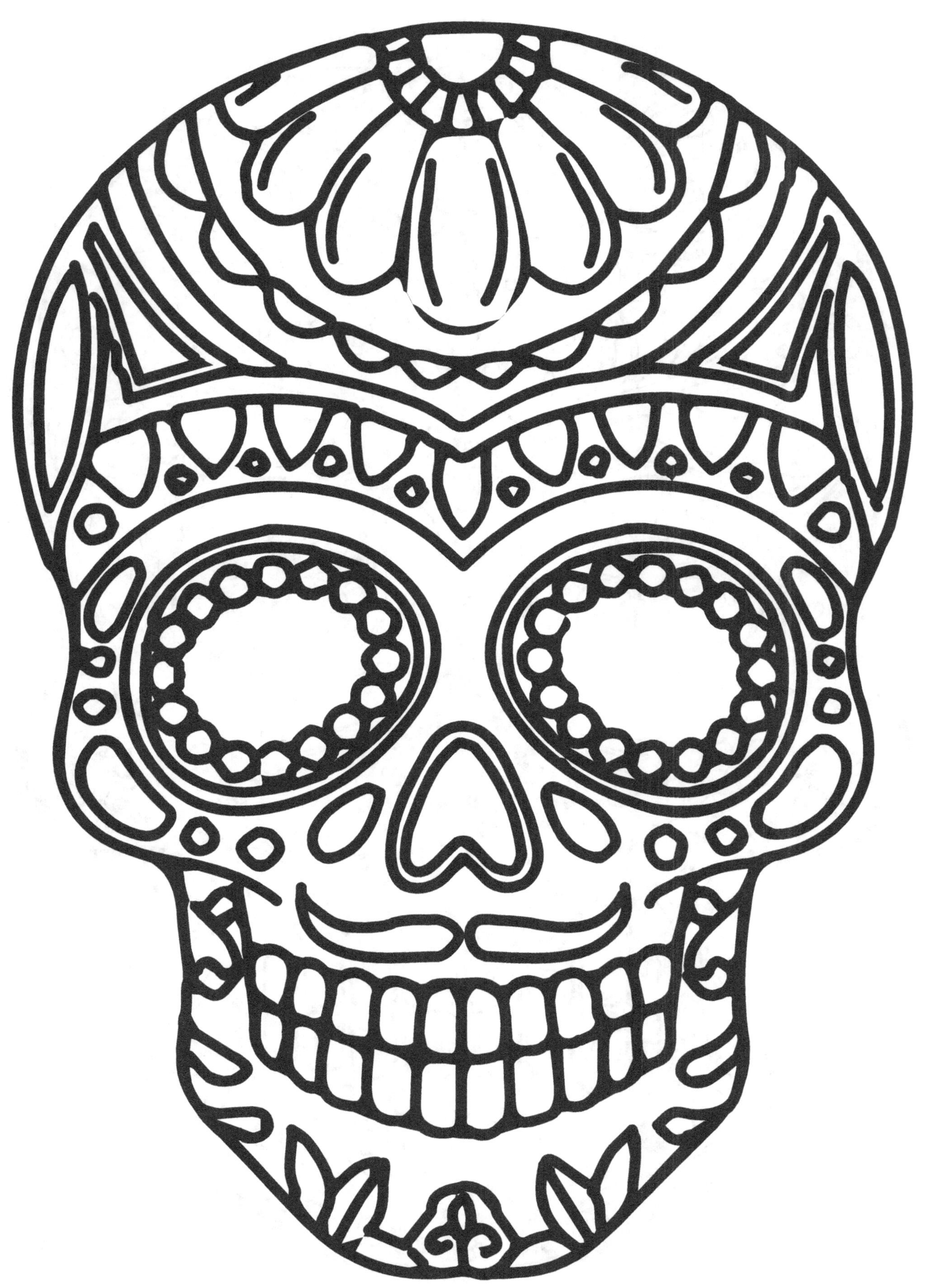

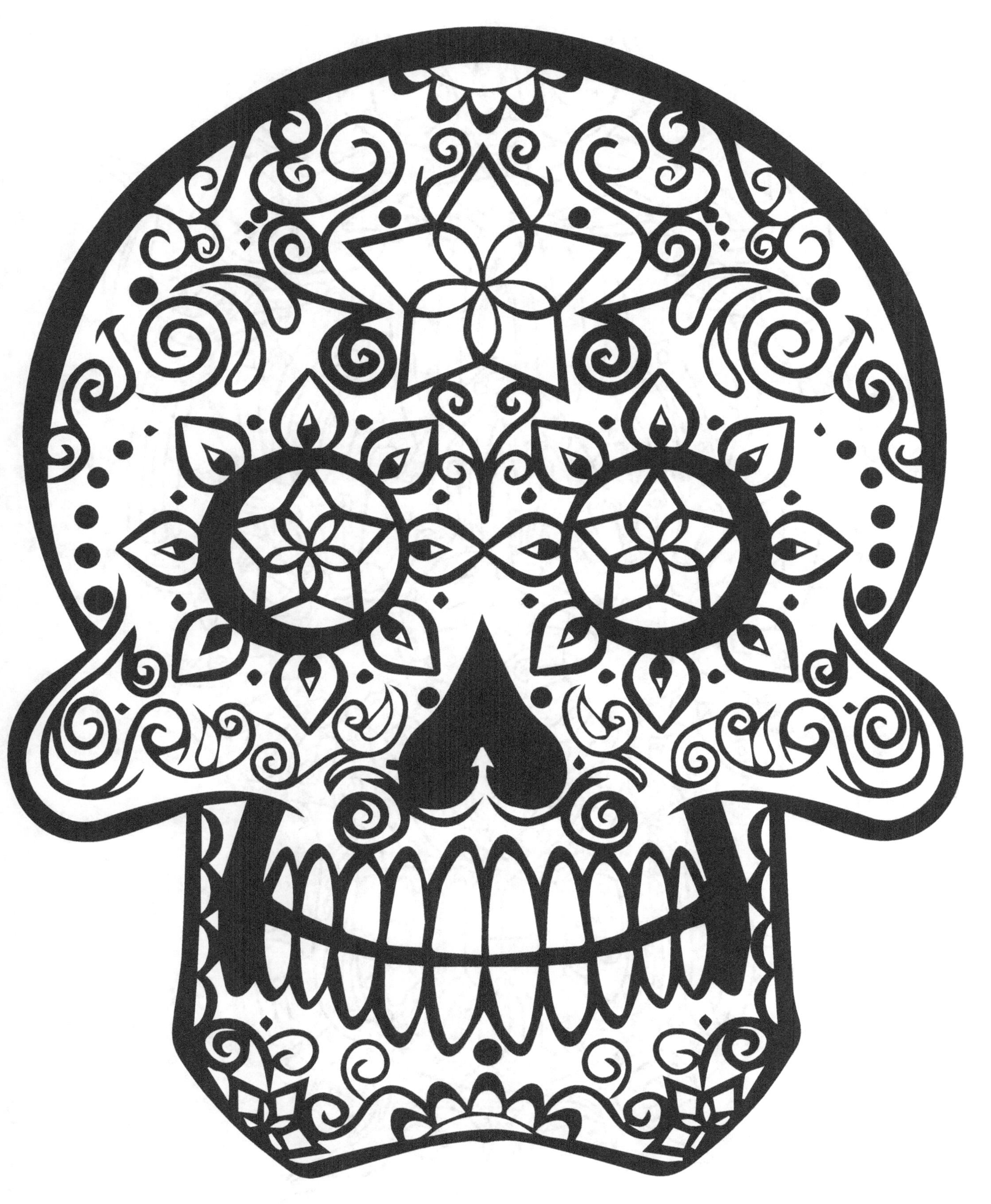

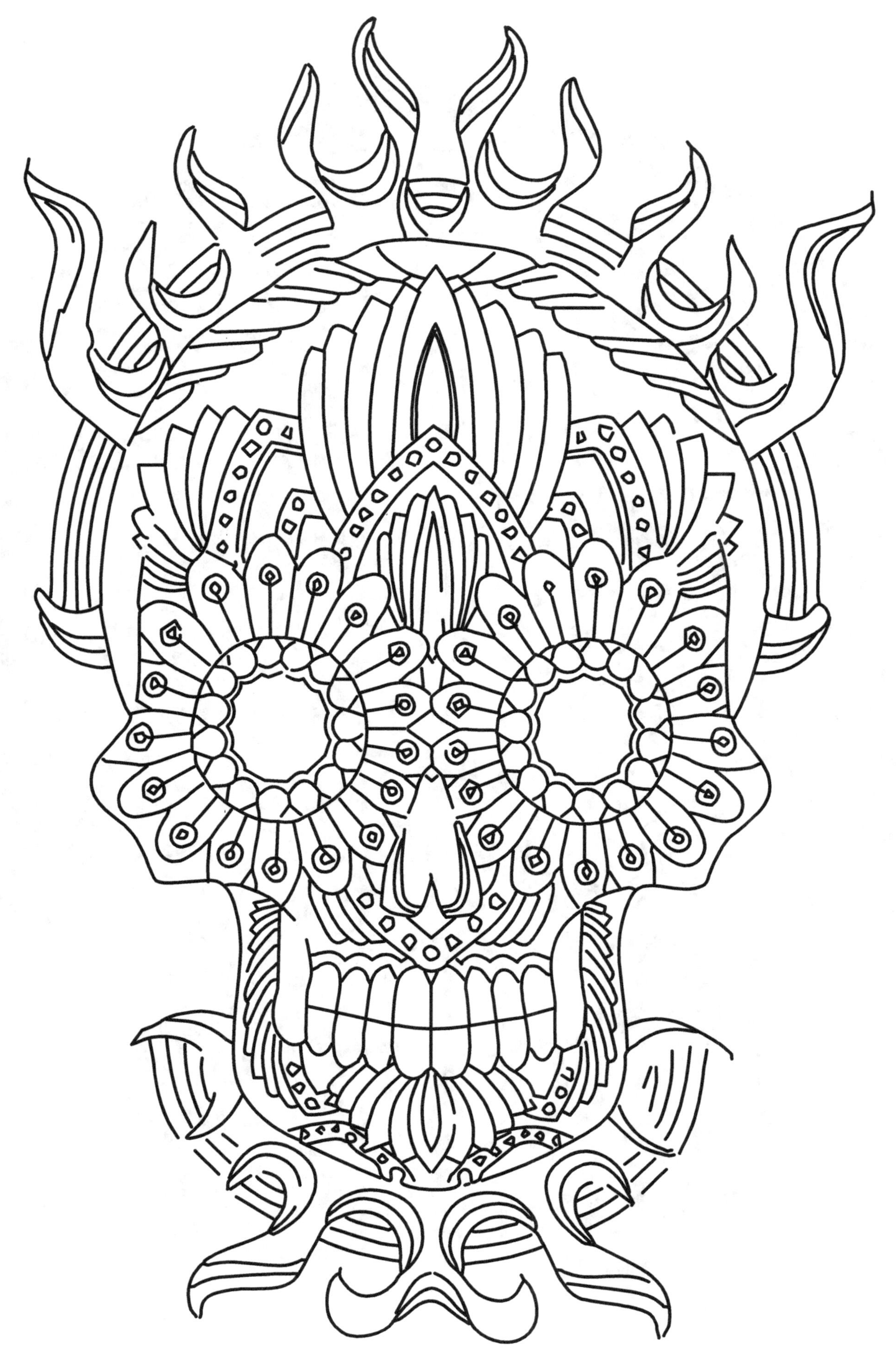

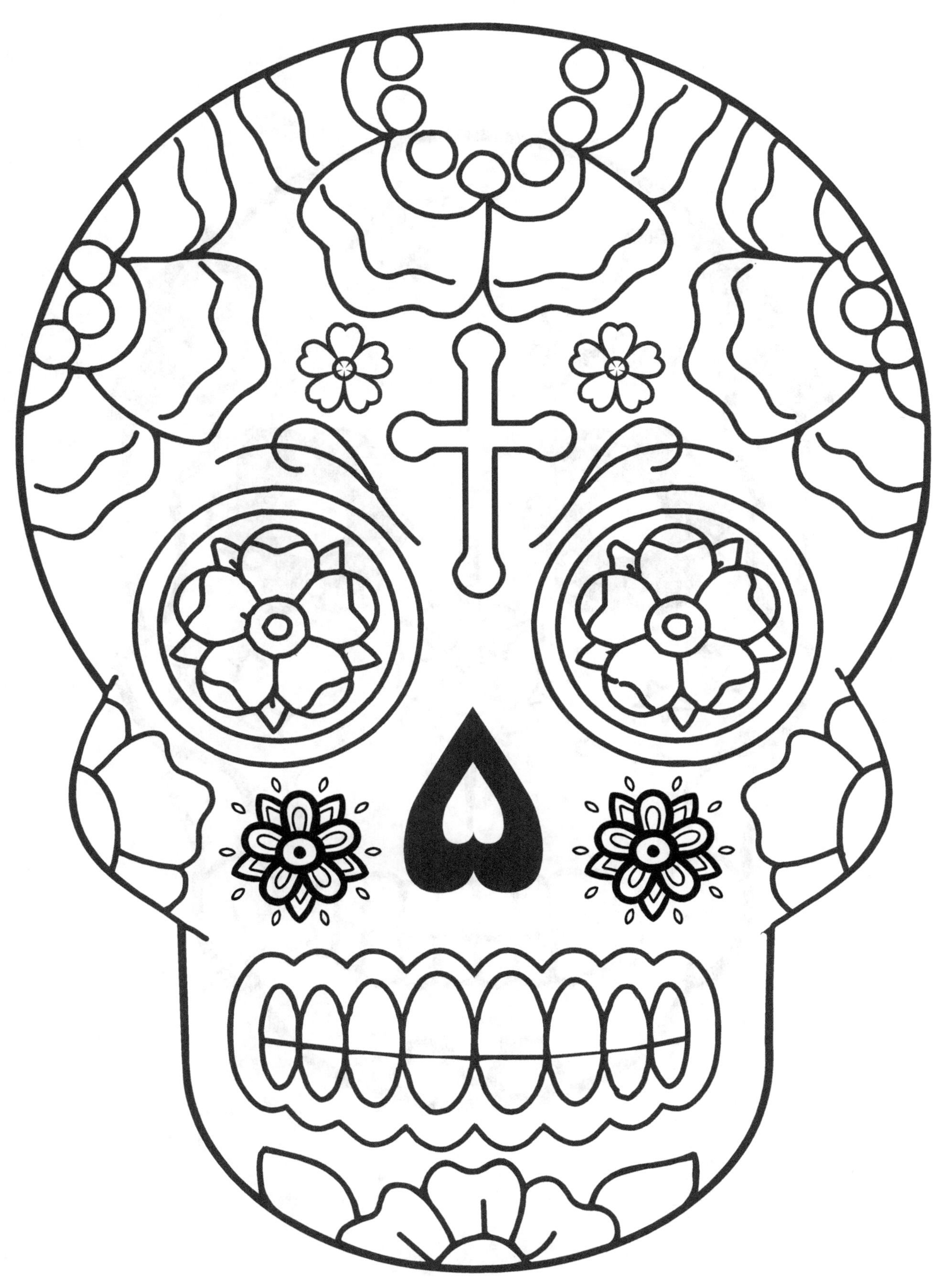

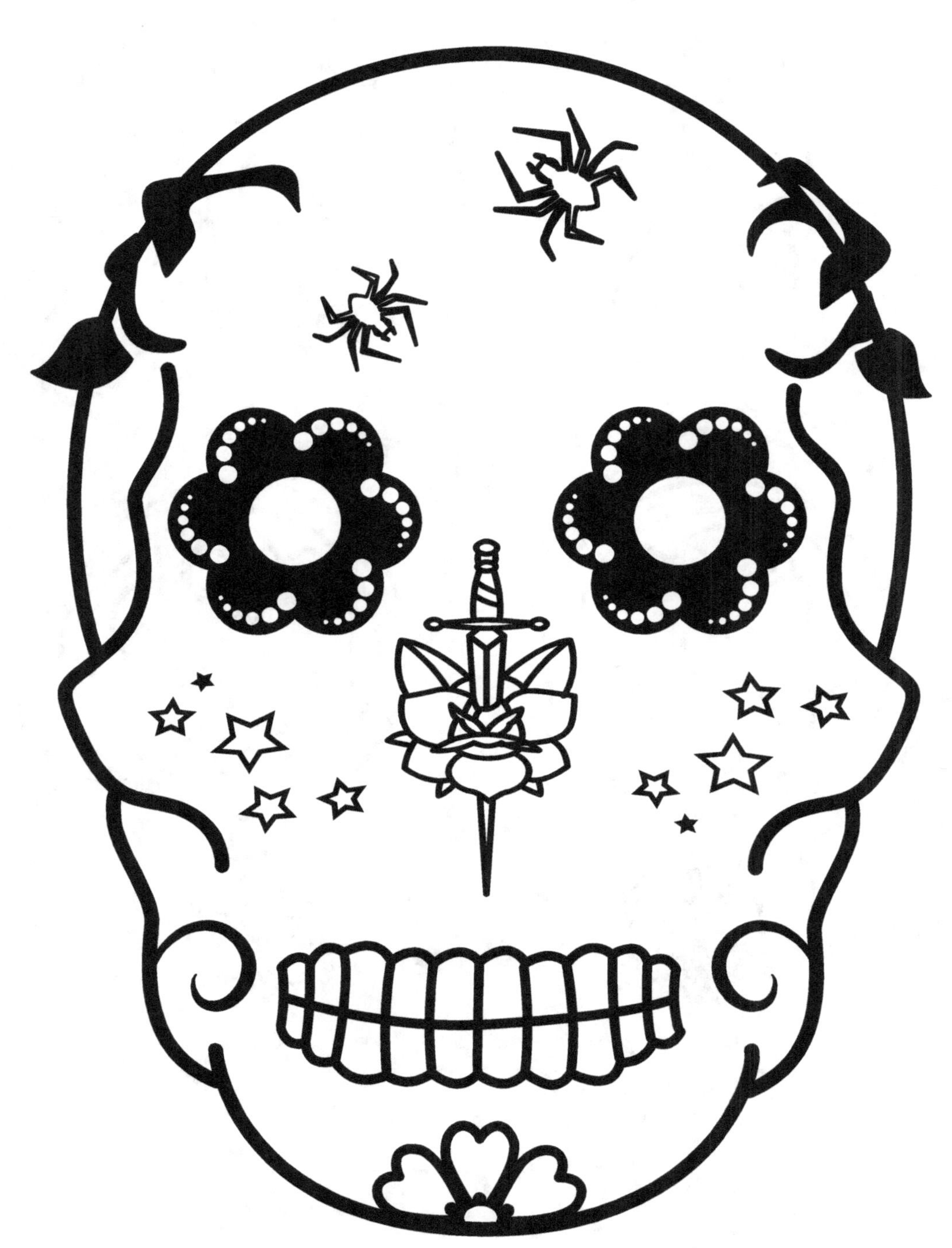

THANK YOU FOR CHOOSING THIS COLORING BOOK,
WE JUST ASK YOU TO SUPPORT US BY GIVING US
A GOOD REVIEW.